Chess on the Web

Sarah Hurst,
Richard Palliser,
Graham Brown

B.T. Batsford Ltd, *London*

First published in 2000
© Sarah Hurst, Richard Palliser, Graham Brown 2000

ISBN 0 7134 8602 3

British Library Cataloguing-in-Publication Data.
A catalogue record for this book is
available from the British Library.

Printed in Great Britain by
Creative Print and Design (Wales), Ebbw Vale
for the publishers,
B.T. Batsford Ltd,
9 Blenheim Court,
Brewery Road,
London N7 9NT

A member of the Chrysalis Group plc

A BATSFORD CHESS BOOK

Contents

*This book is dedicated to Jimmy, Mark, Jon, Gary
and the staff of Attilio's...The Chess Gang*

Introduction

Welcome to the 2nd edition

The Internet is an incredibly fast-changing medium and a book such as this has to be regularly updated. In the 2nd edition of *Chess on the Web* my co-authors Richard Palliser, Graham Brown, and I have included a great deal of new material, while retaining the most important information from the original book. From the many thousands of chess Websites, newsgroups and electronic mailing lists, we have chosen 133 wonderful, popular, useful, or just plain wacky ones to review, based on our own experience, recommendations from professional and amateur chess players, and Web links. Since the 1st edition, some sites have changed completely, in particular the BCM, BCF, 4NCL and FIDE sites, and their star ratings and reviews have also changed accordingly.

A few excellent sites that were featured in the 1st edition have sadly disappeared down a black hole in cyberspace, notably the 'Dante's Inferno E-Mail Chess Tournament' and the 'Lytham Ex-Files'. On the other hand, some fantastic sites have sprung up in a very short time, including KasparovChess, which may well have created some *.com* millionaire shareholders by the time the next edition of this book comes out. Meanwhile, many old favourites are maintaining their high standards—Chess Archaeology, The

Chess Café, The Correspondence Chess Place, The Internet Chess Club, The Irish Chess Archive, and The Week in Chess. They are to be congratulated for successfully making it from the 20th to the 21st century, and, who knows, maybe they'll be around in the 22nd century too, if The Irish Chess Archive's Mark Orr achieves his aim of inventing a robot to keep Websites going after the demise of their mortal masters.

Getting started

The Internet has revolutionised chess. Players of all standards, from countries as far apart as China and Chile, India and Italy, can now communicate with each other instantaneously and cheaply. On the Internet you can play; watch, download and analyse games; read chess history, news and scurrilous pieces of gossip; join heated debates; buy books, magazines and equipment; solve problems; meet grandmasters; take lessons; watch a chess TV show; and even listen to chess songs. The Internet won't kill off 'real life' chess; on the contrary, it brings a new dimension to the game and must have inspired thousands of newcomers to check out their local club.

There are two main components of the Internet: the World Wide Web, referred to in this book as 'the Web'; and e-mail (electronic mail). A Website can be as simple as a page of text like this one, or it can be a jumpin', jivin', mind-blowing multimedia experience, featuring animated graphics, music, live conversation and video clips. As John Saunders explains in his revealing article, 'Secrets of Webmastery', you need very little technical expertise to set up your own Website. Most Webmasters (Janet Edwards of Barnet is one of the very few chess Webmistresses) taught themselves the skills they needed. The most important characteristics of a Webmaster, dedication and tolerance, can't be taught.

Of course, you don't have to have your own site to appreciate the full glories of the Web. Surfing the net is as easy as learning the moves of chess. If you're not already connected, look in an Internet magazine to find out what deals the Internet service providers (ISPs) are offering. Some, like Dixons' Freeserve in the UK, charge no monthly fee, but their technical support service might be expensive or non-existent. The popular America OnLine (AOL) offers special pages for members, but it might not be the best ISP for you. A recommendation from a friend is as good as anything.

When you have your Internet account up and running, click on the icon which represents your browser (Internet Explorer or Netscape Navigator) and you'll hear the modem dialling, or, if you have an ISDN line, you'll be connected almost instantaneously. A Web page will soon appear, probably the homepage of your ISP. At the top of your screen you'll see a narrow, horizontal window, which contains the address, or URL, of the site. All addresses begin with *http//*, so this prefix has been omitted from the site addresses in this book, as it is taken for granted.

To start looking at chess sites, you could go to a general search engine, such as Yahoo!, by typing in the address: *www.yahoo.com*. Then you can search for a site using a keyword or phrase, 'Barnet chess club', for example. If you type the word 'chess' into a general search engine, you will be presented with hundreds of thousands of sites where there is a mention of the word.

If you know the address of a particular chess site then you can just type it straight in, but if you just feel like browsing, then the simplest way is to go to a links site, such as InternetChess.com (*www.Internetchess.com*). There you'll find a huge list of chess sites grouped into categories, and you can get to each site by clicking on its name. Sites that you really like can be added to 'Favourites', so that you can return to them again and again without having to type in the address or go via a links site.

The other component of the Internet, e-mail, comes as a package with your Internet account. Your ISP will give you instructions on how to choose an e-mail address, such as *sarah.hurst@btInternet.com*, and many accounts entitle you to multiple e-mail addresses so that you can use one for work and one for chess, if you like. Again, favourite addresses can be stored in an electronic address book so that you don't have to look them up. It is also possible to create a free e-mail account on the Web with Hotmail or Yahoo! These services are time-consuming to access, because each message is stored on a separate Web page, but the advantage is that you can check your mail on any computer in the world with an Internet connection.

Apart from sending and receiving individual e-mails, you can also subscribe to newsgroups and mailing lists. These are discussion forums in which conventional rules of spelling and grammar are rarely adhered to. Some people never use capital letters. Common symbols are :) which is a smiley face and :(which is an unhappy face. Some discussion groups are moderated, which means unpleasant messages aren't published, but many are unmoderated and may cause offence. A discussion group's code of conduct may be sent to you when you subscribe, and is known as 'netiquette'.

The difference between mailing lists and newsgroups is that messages from mailing lists are sent directly to your personal e-mail box, while newsgroups are kept in separate files. You can download messages from newsgroups whenever you like, and if you don't look at a newsgroup for a few weeks or months, old messages will be deleted and you will never see them. Messages from mailing lists come to you automatically, so you might receive several in a day. If you're planning to be away from your computer for more than a week, it's best to suspend your subscription or unsubscribe from mailing lists temporarily, so that you don't find hundreds of unwanted messages waiting when you get back.

What's in this book

Reviews of many more sites, newsgroups and mailing lists have been added since the 1st edition of *Chess on the Web*, whilst some have been removed, either because a site no longer exists or because it hasn't been updated for a long time. Each site reviewed has a rating from one to five stars, with one star meaning poor, two stars mediocre, three stars average, four stars very good and five stars excellent. Standards vary from chapter to chapter: in the 'Where to Play' chapter, it is very difficult to attain a five-star rating because of the standard set by the Internet Chess Club, while in the 'Archives and Databases' chapter, it is difficult to find fault with the numerous sites which offer thousands of free games to download.

More than one-third of the sites reviewed in this edition have received five-star ratings, but that doesn't mean that the calibre of chess sites on the Internet is unusually high. Sites have been chosen for review because they advertised themselves well, or because they were recommended on a links site. Less well-known sites are probably languishing in obscurity for a good reason. Sites that are not written in English have been left out, although many bilingual or multilingual sites have been reviewed. Sites devoted to a particular locality, such as Mitcham chess club, haven't been reviewed unless they are particularly unusual or offer something that would appeal to a wider audience.

Most spelling and grammatical errors have been left uncorrected in the quotes and extracts from Websites, to give an impression of the site's style. If the English is unintelligible, that is usually a good indicator that the quality of the site is not high. In the 'Headers' section of reviews, the most important headings on a site's homepage have been listed (most of which lead to another page), but the 'Links' and 'E-mail us' headers have been left out because they appear on nearly every site. In the 'Pricecheck' section, a selection of popular products such as Fritz6 and Batsford's *Modern Chess Openings*, along with items that can only be purchased on a particular site, have been chosen from the often vast online shopping malls.

The 'Webmaster Hall of Fame' is a selection of interviews (conducted by e-mail!) with the Webmasters of five-star sites. Not all the Webmasters of five-star sites could be interviewed, but this is a representative sample. Those interviews which appeared in the 1st edition of *Chess on the Web* and were worthy of inclusion again have been updated, and some new ones have been added. In the 'Best of the Web' section you can read some of the most interesting articles from chess sites. All the extracts from the 1st edition have been replaced with new ones. There are no extracts from sites whose Webmasters are in the Hall of Fame, because this book aims to give a flavour of as many different sites as possible. We have also tried to select articles that are short, and that appear exclusively on the Web—not articles that were put on the Web from books or magazines.

A word of warning: content changes very quickly on the Internet, so the reviews only reflect the sites as they were at the time of writing. Web addresses may also have changed, but if the site still exists, it should be possible to find it via a links site or search engine.

Acknowledgements

Thanks to all those Webmasters and Internet users who answered our questions, gave permission for their articles to be reproduced and offered advice on which sites to review. Special thanks to John Saunders for revealing the secrets of Webmastery, and to my parents for all the printing and support—edible, technical and moral.

Sarah Hurst, Beijing, August 2000

1
Megasites

Some websites are just too big to be slotted into individual categories. Being big doesn't necessarily make them the best sites for playing, or history, or analysis, because they are non-specialist. But they certainly have a great deal to offer and are ideal places to start exploring the world of chess on the web.

A/ Webmaster Hall of Fame
'Mig' (Michael Greengard), KasparovChess.com

Please introduce yourself

Mig Greengard. (Mig being short for Miguel and not my initials!) Since July 1999, I have been the Vice-President in charge of content of KasparovChess Online Inc. and the editor-in-chief of *KasparovChess.com*. Previously I wrote about chess for several websites and magazines in my spare time and ran my own consulting business in Argentina. I am originally from California, but until my recent return to the US, I had lived in Latin America for over eight years.

How strong a chess player are you, and do you play on KC?

I haven't had time to play in a serious tournament in years, but I'm around master strength based on results against

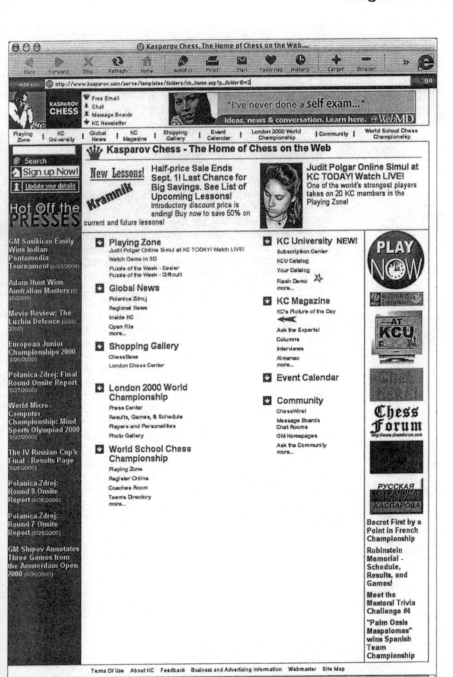

international masters and grandmasters in online play and blitz. Working in and around chess full-time for a few years has improved my play by osmosis, but Garry can still give me two pawns! I play at KC practically every day and we're getting stronger players all the time. Actually, even the beginner chess players in the NY office have become addicted.

How did the KC team get together and when?

It was a multi-phase project that could take a long time to explain. At the beginning of 1999, Garry launched the 'Club Kasparov' website in Moscow, written primarily in Russian. Then investors were brought aboard and the creation of a new company and a new, modern site was started simultaneously in New York and Herzlia, Israel in early 1999. Several of the business people in NY and developers in Israel had started working on the project before there was even an office! Most of this original technical team was formed under the guidance of Mr Shay Bushinsky, a friend of Garry's, and also one of the programmers of the Junior computer program. The development office in Israel—which also produces content to take advantage of the many talented GMs in Israel—currently has a staff of around 30.

For me it was a little more curious and it all began with an early-morning phone call from Garry Kasparov to my home in Buenos Aires, Argentina in June 1999. Suddenly I was being offered a job leading the content team of this amazing new chess website with unprecedented funding and technical resources. And to work with the World Champion! How could I say no? Three weeks later I arrived in Israel, where I spent almost seven months working with the developers and forming an international content team that now has over 30 members. When the site went live, I was off to the Big Apple.

The New York office was formed as the executive and business development base. We wanted top professionals in these areas and they were hired by recruiters in the marketing and finance fields. KC also has an expanding education department in New York led by Michael Khodarkovsky, an old friend and trainer of Garry's. We also have a small office in London where we recruit instructors for our multimedia lessons. Moscow is still the primary content centre and our team of trainers, writers, and journalists there is around 16 people.

Why did you move to New York?

It does seem strange that I would move around so much in an Internet business, but it was important to have someone from the heart of the development and content here in NY with the business and finance guys. Success in the USA is critical for the success of the company and the USA is still where the biggest block of Internet users are, and, equally important, where most of the venture capital is to be found. To be successful, we have to integrate the development and content of the site with the marketing and funding of the company as a whole.

How much involvement in the website does Kasparov have, and what is he like to work with?

Garry is very involved at all levels. He takes an active interest in everything from raising capital to the organisation of the World School Chess Championships, from the layout of the website to the services we offer our members. It's his name on the door and he likes to know that we are keeping the quality high. It was a little surprising to see the interest he takes and how fast he picks things up. Suddenly he's participating in conversations about Java applets and server stability!

I'm not trying to make him out to be a Superman or a busy-body; but he knows a lot about every area of the site and he enjoys participating. Many excellent content ideas were suggested by Garry personally. He knows the chess world and chess fans very well and adds a lot more than his name to the site. I know everybody likes to think he's looking over the editors' shoulders and every word on the site comes from him, but he's been very hands-off regarding the politics and editorial content.

It won't surprise anyone to hear he is very intense to work with. He concentrates fully on just about anything presented him so you have to be on your toes and have your facts straight the first time. He has a knack for asking the exact question you don't have the answer to. The first thing I thought, and this is what I hear from many who meet him for the first time, is that it's amazing he also plays chess! He seems totally absorbed in these other things, like chess in schools or the website; it's hard to believe he's not only a full-time chess player, but perhaps the best of all time.

Have you ironed out the problems experienced during the Cadet Grand Prix and Inaugural Grand Prix, and do you intend to hold regular Internet events such as these?

I'm not sure technical problems are ever completely ironed out, it's just the nature of these complicated systems. We have certainly come a long, long way since those two events, both held at the beginning of 2000 in our 'beta' days. We bit off more than we could chew and were all really suffering back then. Because of those problems we had a moratorium on professional events until we could get things in order. But despite the technical problems both events were immensely popular and we are already planning several new professional events. We haven't changed our opinion that the future of professional chess is online and, of course, at *KasparovChess.com.*

Which GMs play on the site regularly?

We have a few regulars, plus we've had some special guests like Judit Polgar, and of course, Garry Kasparov. GMs Bareev, Har-Zvi, Golubev, and Janovsky come in to play members, which gives anyone a chance to play a grandmaster.

Which websites are your main competitors, and are there any chess sites or chess publications which you would like to emulate?

I suppose we have competition in various forms on the web, but really there is nobody out there creating a comprehensive chess supersite like KasparovChess. There are quite a few other places to play, like Yahoo!, FICS (Free Internet Chess Server) and the ICC (Internet Chess Club), which is a pay site. Then there are many with chess news, others with instruction, but nobody close to having it all like we do. It's mostly a question of resources. You can either search around 20 different sites or find it all at KC.

I'm not sure I'd say we are trying to emulate anyone, mostly because our target audience is quite different from most of the sites out there now. News sites like 'The Week In Chess' and playing servers like the ICC are completely targeted toward the serious chess hobbyists and professionals. While we have more than enough for that audience at KC, we are the first to try to reach groups like casual players and parents and kids.

How much feedback do you get from visitors to the site, and what are their main criticisms/aspects that they particularly like?

There is certainly no shortage of feedback! We get around 50 messages per day on average. Most of the criticism lately has been about problems with our live event coverage, still an imperfect science. And we have so much content—over 200 pages a month—that navigation issues are a source of many complaints. People are often surprised to find some of the great stuff we have buried in the site! The most popular section of the site is always KasparovChess University (KCU), our downloadable multimedia lessons. People are amazed to be able to take a lesson from a GM in their home. Our on-site news reporting, with an emphasis on analysis and photos, is also very popular. Oh, and the 'Ask the Experts' section is remarkable. We have experts all over the world answering hundreds of questions submitted by readers; it's probably my favourite section to read.

What are you aiming to do with KC Magazine, what does it have to offer that is different from a printed magazine, and is there anything that you wouldn't publish?

KC Magazine is a catch-all for all the content that isn't current news, and includes a lot of instructional material as well as book reviews and interviews. My aim is to turn it into a repository of chess knowledge that becomes the definitive source. The almanac, the sections on openings and endings, is like getting a dozen new chess books every month. The challenge is to organize all the information and catalogue it so people can use it.

The biggest advantages we have over print magazines are those of space, technology, and timeliness. We don't have page limits, so if we have a 7-page theoretical article from Sveshnikov, we can run it. And we can include supplementary games in an online viewer with notes, so the reader doesn't have to set up a board. If we do an interview with Kramnik about his play in Dortmund, it runs the day after the tournament finishes, instead of two months later like in a print magazine.

I don't believe in censorship of any sort, decisions along those lines are based on what our readers would find interesting and that's the bottom line. But political rumours and hearsay have no place at *KasparovChess.com*, unless it is clearly marked as such. Because we are the premier chess site, we have a certain responsibility to verify facts and to check things out before publishing them. This means other sites might be first sometimes, but we'll be right!

Who are your most popular contributors?

Well, Garry Kasparov is pretty popular! He sends in 'Express Commentary' on the same day as his games and that's always the most popular material on the site. Several of our regional editors are talented and entertaining writers, including GM Jonathan Levitt in England, Chris Depasquale in Australia, and Jan van de Mortel in Holland. We also have analysis and commentary from many GMs and I hear a lot of good things about Sergey Shipov and Ronen Har Zvi. They both make chess commentary entertaining and informative for players of all levels.

At the moment you seem to be providing all your services for free and depending on advertising revenue. Is that likely to change?

No, that's our model and the site will remain free. Apart from advertising we have many other revenue sources. In July, 2000, we are launching a subscription service version of KasparovChess University that we believe will be very successful. We also do profit-sharing with the stores in our shopping gallery and that will continue to expand. KC will also have its own merchandise, and who wouldn't want a KasparovChess chessboard or sweatshirt?!

According to the ICC, KC wants to buy the 'rights' to show big events live, but no legal procedure has been established for this yet. Is that really your intention and how would it work?

We have already done this and it's not according to anyone but us! We announced it to the world, it's not some diabolical conspiracy. We purchased exclusive live broadcast rights to the Dortmund 2000 supertournament that just finished and we will continue to invest in professional chess in this way. KasparovChess Online signed a contract with the organisers to be the exclusive source of live coverage, meaning other sites (like the ICC) were not allowed to show the games while they were in progress. This brings in a lot of money for the organisers—and therefore the players—and I hope this will become standard in chess as it is in every other sport. It's just another step toward chess becoming a true professional sport. There should be bidding for the rights like there is in every other sport.

I'm no expert on the legal procedures involved, which is why lawyers are taking over our part of the world as well! It has to do with the games in progress being 'time-sensitive information' and protected like the television broadcast of a football match.

What are your future plans for the site?

We have many plans, it's more a question of priorities. It's hard to decide what to do first. We are doing extensive work on the Playing Zone to have more member activities like tournaments and contests. Now that the core functionality is good, we're doing a lot of cosmetic work on all areas. Soon the Kids' Corner will launch and that is going to be amazing. A major area of expansion will be live lessons and lectures at KasparovChess University, something that is already very popular. This year's edition of the World School Chess Championship is going to take a lot of time and resources and will be a major part of the site in the final months of 2000. In all, we will continue to make KasparovChess.com the definitive source for chess in the world.

B/ Best of the Web

Who is Who

1) Peter Svidler

What is your personal understanding of the beauty of chess?

There is no difference between chess and other arts: one cannot confuse a beautiful game with an ordinary one, but there is no precise definition of beauty, in my opinion.

What game of yours do you consider to be the best?

Shirov-Svidler, Tilburg, 1997.

What game in chess history made the most impression on you?

I can mention two or three such games for every age: from Morphy-Consultants and Anderssen-Kieseritzky to the 24th game of the match of the year 1985, with all its stops.

How do you use chess software? Any quick tip for an average player?

Mostly for opening studies.

How often do you play online? What place do you prefer?

I play on the ICC.

How do you see the future of chess on the web?

I see it bright.

2) Sergey Ivanov

These questions are of a global character and require full-length, detailed answers, yet I'll try to be concise.

What is your personal understanding of the beauty of chess?

I comprehend the beauty of chess as a symbiosis of investigations and analytical work at home, with improvisation and creative work when playing at the board. Most beautiful games in the history of chess have appeared as a result of an accumulation of previous knowledge and experience, combined with inspiration, leading to a chess player's emotional breakthrough during play.

What game of yours do you consider to be the best?

To be honest, I haven't yet thought about writing memories and issuing a game collection. But, based on my understanding of the beauty of chess (see above), I consider those games in which these two basic elements are well combined, to be my best.

I can point to two of my recent games:

1) Aseev K.-Ivanov S (St Petersburg, 1997)

Played in the Tournament of City Fellows. I managed to find and fulfill a stunning idea in a well-known line of the Botvinnik variant: 22...♖h5!!. Black sacrifices one rook, then another, and his four passed pawns prove to be equal in the struggle against two rooks! By the way, this game came fifth in the 69th book of *Chess Informant's* list of greatest games.

2) Ivanov S.-Mikhalevski V. (St Petersburg, 1999)

Played in the second unofficial match against the Beer-Sheba team. I succeeded in restoring to life a rejected line in a popular variant of the Gruenfeld Defence, developing a well-based attacking plan (16 f5!) and mating the opponent's king. The game is published on the site of the GrandMaster Chess School.

What game in chess history made the most impression on you?

M. Botvinnik was my idol when I was a boy (he still is). I liked his logical approach to play very much. I consider the famous game, Botvinnik-Capablanca (AVRO Tournament, 1938), his greatest chess triumph. Consistent realisation of a plan was finished off with a combination burst (30 ♗a3!).

As for beautiful tactical struggles, the game Polugayevsky-Nezhmetdinov (Sochi, 1958) impressed me the most: the white king went from g1 to a5 and was mated, when the board was still full of pieces!

Regarding endgames, the position from the game Ortueta-Sanz is engraved in my memory, when White's rook and knight were helpless against Black's separated pawns.

How do you use chess software? Any quick tip for an average player?

I use chess software very intensively. I use data bases, chiefly ChessBase, and less often, Chess Assistant—to prepare for tournaments and particular opponents, to comment on my own and others' games, to write articles, to place my materials on the web, etc. For analysis purposes, I use analytical modules, such as Fritz 6. Sometimes I play with chess programs just for fun.

How often do you play online? What place do you prefer?

I don't play online. Firstly, I have just no time for this, and, secondly, they mainly play blitz or rapid chess on the web, while I prefer playing with classical time control. Yet, it seems to me that everybody is playing at ICC now, so I feel like going to try too!

How do you see the future of chess on the web?

The Internet is a very good medium for the promotion and popularisation of chess. One can very quickly find the required information on the web. Not only can you play chess with partners of practically every level, but you can also teach and learn chess, take and give lessons, prepare and study theoretical surveys, and do many other things.

Internet tournaments are very interesting as well, at least they can replace correspondence chess. Still, one should not run to extremes here: personal contests are very necessary too, as there are not just advantages, but shortcomings too in the absence of an opponent. Besides, trips to tournaments help chess players to establish new relationships, bring them new impressions, etc. Thus, I consider the future of chess to be a combination of analysis and play at the chessboard, with the possibilities provided by the Internet.

3) Eugeny Solozhenkin

What is your personal understanding of the beauty of chess?

The sense of chess consists for me in the victory of strategic laws over malicious intent, ignorance, lack of education and adventurism. Beauty springs up from such a victory, whether it comes as integral positional play, a tremendous attack with sacrifices, or a heroic defence.

What game of yours do you consider to be the best?

This is a good question for a person who has finished his career. I have played a number of games I am proud of, but, really, I find it difficult to pick one out and mark it down as the very best. The one that I chose is significant for me because its subject and its final position remind me of a game that struck me when I was a child, Solozhenkin-Lupu (Parthenay, 1992).

What game in chess history made the most impression on you?

> Alekhine-Nimzowitsch (San-Remo, 1930). For a child playing at second or third class, it was a shock: a zugzwang in the middlegame instead of the endgame.

How do you use chess software? Any quick tip for an average player?

> I use ChessBase mainly, as a source of information.

How often do you play online? What place do you prefer?

> Not very often. Yahoo! and ICC.

How do you see the future of chess on the web?

> How about writing a virus called 'I love chess'? This would block a computer's work until its user solved a mate in one— just to enhance the prestige of chess!

> *GrandMaster Chess (www.gmchess.com)*

C/ Websites

1) Chessworld.net ****

> Headers: *Latest, News, Chatting, Learning, Culture, Kasparov, Shopping, Gamezone, Downloads, Playing, Computer, Grading, Reports, Guest GM, Contest, Drama, Club focus, Feedback*

> Having started out as the home in cyberspace of Barnet Chess Club in North London, this site appears to be perpetually expanding, like the universe. There is a great deal of material here, much of it lightweight, but on the whole very entertaining and sometimes educational. Webmaster Tryfon Gavriel and webmistress Janet Edwardson, are spreading their skills a little thinly, though. As a result, the site is rather disorganised, without a clear purpose.
> At the highest level there are the well-known 'Coffee Break Chess' columns by GM Alexander Baburin from Ireland (see chapter 3—Analysis). Then there are games with annotations by the Chessworld.net team, such as the incredible Kasparov vs. Topalov, from the 1999 Hoogevens tournament in Wijk aan Zee. On the historical side, there are articles with photographs and illustrations on Steinitz, Capablanca, Alekhine (accompanied by appropriate classical music) and various famous matches including Fischer-Spassky 1972— material which was mainly culled from the TV programme 'Clash of the Titans'.

For news of big events, Chessworld.net directs visitors to coverage on other sites, but has its own reports on events in Britain. One particularly useful feature on the site is the 'Chess Clubs Worldwide!' section, where you can search for information about clubs, chess federations and events, by clicking on a region or a country. The Belarus page, for example, has links to the Belarus Chess Federation, the Belarus Championship 2000 and Ukrainian tournaments in March 2000—which isn't Belarus, but close! On the Antarctica Chess page, the anticipation soon turns to disappointment, when intrigued visitors are greeted with the message, "Any Igloos with Internet connections wishing to be added here, please e-mail".

In terms of learning, Chessworld.net offers some Nimzo-Indian and Queen's Gambit Declined learning papers as well as a collection of over 2,000 Smith-Morra games to download. You can also test yourself in the fun quizzes (tactics and history) and read the weird and wonderful philosophical treatises such as "Re-assess your chess happiness." In this paper chess players are urged to enjoy the moment and stop being so obsessed with their grading: "If your happiness in chess is qualified by the future, then you may think to yourself that you will never be a Grandmaster. Therefore you will always be a bunny or a fish. But so what? You may find yourself turning down opportunities to play for your local club, because your grading went down from last year, and you cannot be bothered any more with chess. Instead why don't you forget your chess ambitions for the future and just concentrate on really enjoying every game of chess you play."

Despite the headers 'Gamezone' and 'Playing', you can't actually play on this site—both sections advise you to try other sites such as the Internet Chess Club. On the other hand, if you are here to find out about Barnet Chess Club, Chessworld.net tells you everything you could possibly need to know, including a map of the vicinity around the clubhouse, reports on epic clashes with local teams and downloads of the games of Barnet's top players (Natasha Regan, honorary member, IM Neil Bradbury, Paul Georghiou and Alex Ethelontis).

If you have thoughts to share with other visitors to Chessworld.net, a website to plug, a used car to sell, or a query that you think chess players can help you with, post a message in the Forum. Here, somebody called Warner complains about chess frustration: "Hi, I started to play chess rather intensively a year ago, I attended some sessions at a chess club, then bought a chess program and began to play against it. I also played a lot online, on Yahoo! Subsequently, my rating started to slowly rise, from 1200 to 1300. I even bought a CD-ROM, on opening theory, and studied some ECO-openings that I encountered during my chess sessions.

But suddenly, during the last weeks, my playing became worse and worse, and I lost many games against lower rated players. Thus I dropped back, to around 1240. I am pretty fed up with chess at the moment, even when I find it generally fascinating... Has anyone had similar experiences? Any hints how I could overcome my 'chess-crisis'?" W. Donalds wants to know if Paul Morphy ever played the Muzio Gambit, Dr Cyril Josephs wants to know how the rook got its name (to tell his class of young, gifted children) and Rob Kruszynski points out that the site omitted Tigran Petrosian from its line-up of world champions, making Kasparov the 12th instead of the 13th.

A glaring error which demonstrates that Chessworld.net is struggling in certain areas—sometimes less is more, and perhaps Gavriel and Edwardson should concentrate on making this a top-notch club site instead of attempting to do everything.

2) GrandMaster Chess *****
www.gmchess.com

Headers: *FIDE, General, Local, Analysis, Lectures, Special services, Feature articles, Magazine, Game-bases, Tournament calendar, Club pages, Books, Software, Equipment, Blah-blah place* Pricecheck: *Express Analysis US$29.95, M. Tal. Games 1949-1962 $23.95, Chess Assistant 5.0 $138.95*

You wouldn't stake too much on FIDE World Champion Alexander Khalifman beating Garry Kasparov in a chess match, but their respective websites are certainly jostling for position at the top of the ratings table. GrandMaster Chess is the site of Khalifman's chess school in St Petersburg, which opened in 1998. The team that runs the school and the website is remarkably strong, including GMs Gennady Nesis (runner-up in the 11th World Correspondence Chess Championship), Peter Svidler (three times Russian champion), Konstantin Sakaev (one-time Russian champion), Vladimir Epishin (long-term official second of Anatoly Karpov), Evgeny Solozhenkin (one-time St Petersburg champion), Konstantin Aseev (winner of several international tournaments) and Sergei Ivanov (three times St Petersburg champion). The site provides details of how you can enroll in one of the St Petersburg summer schools, or, more conveniently for most, receive training by e-mail. Chess lectures are published on the site so that visitors can get an idea of what they would be signing up to. These are undoubtedly helpful, but they would be vastly improved with the addition of some diagrams with moving pieces.

GrandMaster Chess only occasionally makes use of the full multimedia potential of the Internet, notably for the 'Position of the day', which appears initially as a small diagram in the corner of the screen, but if you click on it you get a full-screen version. Here you can view a brilliant move, after reading comments and trying to guess what happened next. A more in-depth look at games can be found in the 'Analysis' section, where the school's resident experts annotate their own masterpieces—again, a few diagrams wouldn't go amiss here, as it's quite heavy going. Hundreds of recent games from Russian and international tournaments can be downloaded in the FIDE section, where you will also find cross tables, results, links to the websites of big chess events and FIDE press releases.

Thousands more games by living and dead players are available for download in the 'Game-bases' section, including, for example: 1,476 Adams games, 2,725 Karpov games, 3,759 Korchnoi games, 990 Lasker games and 2,554 Tal games, with more being added all the time. Details of forthcoming events are listed in the tournament calendar and the ELO rating of any player in the world can also be checked on the site.

There is a growing archive of feature articles on the site on all sorts of topics: from the pros and cons of the knockout system; to the mystery of the missing match regulations for the encounter between Lasker and Schlechter in 1910; to analysis (with diagrams!) from *Shakhmatniy Peterburg*, St Petersburg's local chess magazine. Apart from anything else, it's great that this website keeps English-speaking enthusiasts in touch with the Russian chess scene. The club pages offer a lively description of the various clubs in St Petersburg and in future there is going to be more information and news from clubs around the world. In the 'Blah-blah' section, the website team sparked off a discussion about the merits of the FIDE world championship knockout system as opposed to the traditional match format, which was quickly joined by visitors to the site.

The content on this site is a successful blend of the informative, the educational and the entertaining, presented neatly and professionally. Those who predicted the demise of chess in Russia after the break-up of the Soviet Union might think again after a few visits.

3) KasparovChess.com *****
www.kasparovchess.com or *www.kasparov.com*
Headers: *Online Events, Playing Zone, KC Magazine, Event Calendar, WSCC, KC University, Global News, Shopping Gallery, Community*

Pricecheck: *ChessBase 7 Starter Package DM 299.00/152.88 euros*

Garry Kasparov's more modest Club Kasparov has grandly metamorphosed itself into KasparovChess.com, or KC (definitely not to be confused with KFC!), which was launched in early 2000 with two Internet tournaments: the Cadet Grand Prix and the Inaugural Grand Prix. The Cadet Grand Prix, featuring eight of the strongest junior players in the world, was won by Teymur Radjabov of Baku, Azerbaijan—Kasparov's home city. Technical problems in the Cadet Grand Prix meant that the young players were sometimes kept waiting for hours when a connection went down, and this was all the more frustrating because all the competitors were in different time zones, from the USA to China. Then the main event was staged, with outsider Jeroen Piket defeating Kasparov in the final. The Inaugural Grand Prix was also dogged by technical problems, unfortunately, with the computer Deep Junior losing its match against Michael Adams by forfeit, again because of a lost connection. KC editor-in-chief Mig Greengard had to make a grovelling apology: "This catastrophe is clearly the responsibility of the KasparovChess.com event team—which failed to provide clear rules and documentation to handle such eventualities—and Mickey Adams, Shay Bushinsky and Amir Ban [the Israeli developers of Deep Junior] were the victims of our poor preparation. They, particularly the Junior team, have good reason to be outraged at the misfortune at the hands of fate and our disregard for proper protocol. They have the sincere apologies of the entire KasparovChess.com team, and as editor-in-chief they have my personal apology for allowing such a marvellous opportunity to turn into a disaster through my own negligence. They also have my thanks for having the character and strength to help us instead of punishing us for our neglect."

These ambitious events may not have run entirely according to plan, but nevertheless they put the KC site on the map as one of the biggest planets in chess cyberspace. KC is a playing site AND a news site AND an online magazine AND a shop AND a chess academy. You can even have your own KC e-mail address so that your name is associated permanently with that of the 13th World Champion. There was some good news for the site in the summer of 2000, when Kasparov won a legal battle to use the URL *www.kasparov.com*, which someone else had registered.

The KC site's main fault is its design: too many new windows keep opening up when you click on a link, and there are too many flashing icons on the pages. Sometimes you want to go back to the home page, but you can't, because there's no link on the page you're looking at. Loading up the Java playing interface is time-consuming, but it's a good program and playing on the site is free, although you have to put up with flashing ads for a dating site. There is a 'Main Playing Hall' for everyone from beginners to grandmasters, a 'Just Play Caf?' ("a friendly hang-out for a friendly game"), a 'KC Dojo', where you can get your "chess black belt" by attending classes and lectures, and a 'Full Contact Chess room', where you can play with assistance from chess software.

In the KC University, the 'Learn to Play' section gives easy-to-follow instructions for beginners, illustrated with diagrams. For chess players who want to improve, there are multimedia lessons from the world's top players, coaching and training tips and special educational projects, one of which is called 'Searching for the Future World Champion'. KC also runs a World Schools Chess Championship, between teams of six.

The multimedia lessons are very impressive, with an extensive range to choose from in the categories: Chess Basics, Great Moments, Chess Hall of Fame, GM Arena, Openings, Tactics, Attacks, Endgames and Events Coverage. You download the software and take an audiovisual guided tour, then you have to download each lesson individually, but it doesn't take long. To really appreciate this facility you need a fast modem, otherwise the voice recordings will stop and start jerkily. If you've got the hardware, then you can listen to GMs Boris Alterman or Sofi Polgar in your bedroom, living room or study going through the main ideas in the Sicilian Dragon or Bobby Fischer's greatest games. In contrast to the multimedia lessons, the coaching and training tips are a rather weak effort, with one of Boris Alterman's training tips of the week being two paragraphs long and exceptionally unenlightening: "I think that it's not such a clever choice to study all sorts of openings. Basic chess rules give you real vision on your chess level and your 'chess character'. From this point of view, you can choose which kind of game you prefer: tactical or positional, with many pieces on the board or endgames..." etc., etc.

KC Magazine has historical articles (e.g. Fischer vs. Spassky: World Chess Championship, 1972), humour (e.g. 42 and a Half Great Ways to Annoy Your Opponent), profiles and interviews (e.g. Simen Agdestein and Vladimir Kramnik). In 'Ask the Experts!' there are various sections—Opening Theory, GM Boris Alterman (the Israeli GM answers questions on anything from chess philosophy to the Dragon Variation), Computer Chess, Chess Heritage and Anything and Everything. Questions submitted range from the technical, "I was recently playing in a 5-minute Knockout blitz tournament. One of my opponents touched a pawn. If he moved that pawn, he would have put himself in check. Does he have to move that piece according to the FIDE rules?"; to the trivial, "Who is the oldest chess player that plays in chess competitions?"; to the ridiculous, "In the photos I've seen from the Corus tournament, many of the players are wearing the same thing day after day... why is this?" The KC team replied to the latter, "The only two possible answers that spring to mind from your question are that either the players never change their clothes, or else the photographs were all taken on the same day. I think we shall opt for the second option." Perhaps Kasparov's associates don't know as much about chess players as they think they do!

The Event Calendar is very good indeed and such a service was long overdue on the Internet. It is neatly laid out, with brief descriptions and links to the relevant event sites themselves. It includes matches between top players, international tournaments and famous players' birthdays. You can search the calendar by event type, start date, end date, event name or keywords. Global News presents reports on many of the biggest chess events with photographs, PGN downloads and sometimes even Kasparov's own analysis from a tournament he is playing in.

The KC house style needs to overcome two vices: sycophancy and defensiveness. On the first count, we get comments like, "I asked Garry to answer some questions for our readers which he very graciously provided", and, as a visitor in the 'Feedback' section pointed out, Vishy Anand's victory in the Frankfurt Giants, ahead of Kasparov, was relegated to the bottom right-hand corner of the news page. Objectivity isn't KC's strong point. It's not only the site's managers who are infected with it. You get comments from people like Grantel Gibbs, "FIDE Master and Chess Enthusiast" from Spanish Town, Jamaica, and it's hard to tell whether they're serious or not: "I have seen it all! I am telling you Garri [sic] cannot do anything further to promote the worldwide appeal of the sport than he is doing now. I don't even know how to describe Garri's contribution to this sport! When he played Boris Becker earlier this year, I thought that was the coolest thing ever, especially since it was live on CNN... But to play Sting, one of the most accomplished musical legends in the world and multi-Grammy award singer, surely will be one of the most unforgettable moments in Chess... Well what else can the greatest Chess player ever do to further advance his sport. Maybe initiate World Peace through the sport, or force a Prime Minister or President to resign!!" Meanwhile, E. Daillet, FIDE Master and 1989 French correspondence champion, urges Garry to "be reasonable" and stand for FIDE president, which would "accomplish all our dreams".

As for defensiveness, it really wasn't necessary for Mig to get so affronted by chess journalist, Lev Khariton's article, 'When Chess History Becomes Boring', which praised the site for being "one of the best", but slated an article by Dan Schifrin on the history of the world championships for being too superficial. Mig's response was almost as long as Khariton's article itself, and in any case, surely Dan Schifrin himself should have responded. In general it's usually best to let readers judge for themselves. Mig's arguments are fair, the historical article was aimed at people who know very little about the subject, not for experts like Lev Khariton. But the long-winded debate itself was boring and demonstrated that one of the Internet's strengths can also be a weakness —unlimited space makes editors lazy. Mig could have made his point in one paragraph, and should have.

KC is keen to create a community of chess players who visit the site regularly to play and chat with each other, and that could be the key to its future success. KC members can discuss chess or post notices in various forums: Openings, Analysis, Chess History, Announcements, KasparovChess. com Feedback, General, KasparovChess University and Computer Chess. And if you're completely addicted and need a regular fix of KC when you're too busy to log on to the site, you can also subscribe to the ChessWire biweekly e-mail newsletter.

2
News

The websites of national chess federations and FIDE are included in this chapter alongside general chess news sites. The best site for international news is indisputably Mark Crowther's TWIC, with its up-to-the-minute reports, crosstables, round-by-round results, web TV interviews and comprehensive files of games to download. For an alternative slant on the news, check out the outrageous site belonging to Sam Sloan, the unstoppable scandalmonger who could be termed the first editor of an Internet chess tabloid.

A/ Webmaster Hall of Fame

Mark Crowther, The Week in Chess

Please introduce yourself

My name is Mark Crowther, I'm 34 years old, and I now compile TWIC full-time after recent sponsorship deals. I used to work at Bradford University in their Modern Languages Centre as a librarian/technician.

How serious a chess player are you?

I have played for years and am currently 194 BCF [about 2110] but haven't played a tournament for a long while. I still play Saturday and Tuesday league chess.

When and why did you decide to set up TWIC?

I reported on events on the Internet almost from the start of finding out about it. That was in 1993 after a friend of mine got moves for the Fischer-Spassky II match and Linares 1993. I collected information because I enjoyed following top class chess. I had scrapbooks from foreign papers like *Politika* and also subscribed to magazines like *Die Schachwoche*. I found I knew a little more than the average person on the net and used to post during major tournaments and events. Eventually rather than using the newsgroups every day, I collected the information together for one posting at the weekend. Journalists started sending me information on other events then and it grew from there.

Did you have any technical problems?

The net isn't rocket science. I try and keep it clear and simple as well. The main technical problems are associated with processing the games to put in ratings, and correcting obvious errors in the games such as making players' names consistent.

Where do you get your material from and is there anything you don't publish?

I mostly get it sent. I'm not a great fan of junior chess, but it's usually time constraints that keep the weaker material out. Junior material is very time-consuming because there are normally a lot of non-rated players in the lower groups and lots of players. I used to be a lot more controversial in my writing until I found GMs actually read my stuff! Also I used to be passionate about FIDE politics, but eventually got worn down by it all. It's a fundamentally corrupt organisation and it really isn't possible for people to be elected cleanly.

Did you have any previous experience in journalism before starting TWIC?

None at all. I have tried to improve my writing but it is not something that comes at all easily to me.

How much feedback do you get from readers, and what are their main criticisms/aspects that they particularly like?

I get quite a lot of feedback. Mostly it's just praise. They sometimes ask why I didn't cover this or that.

What has been your biggest scoop?

News travels so quickly on the Internet and other chess sites read mine for the biggest stories. I'm first on a lot of stories and results, but the idea of a scoop doesn't really apply to the Internet.

What is the French link with TWIC TV—do you have some kind of sponsorship deal?

TWIC TV is a French project to which [owner of the London Chess Centre] Malcolm Pein contributes as presenter, and I believe to some of the costs. It's an interesting project which in the long term can only get better with improved speeds of transmission over the Internet.

What have been the highlights on TWIC TV so far and what plans do you have for it?

Interviews with people such as Khalifman and Anand have been the highlights. It's not a programme I personally have any direct input into.

Other than TWIC TV, how has TWIC changed over the past year

I'm covering many more events daily than I used to. John Henderson has been writing reports directly from many of the strongest events with some excellent photos. That's something which will continue. I think the basic idea has worked well and we will look to add features, rather than make fundamental changes.

Have any competitor sites sprung up over the past year or so, and do you see KasparovChess or the revamped BCF or BCM sites as potential threats?

I don't see any one site dominating and that includes my site and KasparovChess. People don't just visit one site but go to a number of places. Competition can only improve the standards all-round. BCM does an excellent job of covering British events. KasparovChess needs to attract users who only occasionally visit chess sites to be a financial success. If they're successful, it has to be good for everyone.

What are your future plans for the site?

We'll continue to try and develop things to get more readers. The site continues to be very popular. We will shortly improve the presentation and add things such as chat and almost certainly a searchable version of the TWIC magazine.

B/ Websites

1) Australian Chess Federation *****
www.auschess.org.au
Headers: *Columns & Opinion, Scoreboard and Events, Ratings & Players, Development, Archives, Administration*

This site has undergone a remarkable transformation in a short period thanks to webmaster Andrew Allen and also to the demise of Chess World Australia, which has passed on its electronic collection of chess newspaper columns to the federation's site. Now the ACF's site is as lively as you would expect from the land of kangaroos and didgeridoos. Attractively designed and easy to navigate, the site contains practically everything you could desire to know about the Australian chess scene, as well as commentary on international developments, such as the commercialisation of FIDE. Results and reports from Australian adult and junior tournaments are provided here, as are rating lists, e-mail addresses of players and chess journalists, and advice on how to run a successful chess club. There is a bulletin board so that visitors to the site can post their own opinions on the state of chess down under.

2) The British Chess Federation ****
www.bcmchess.co.uk
Headers: *What's New, National News, Regional News, ChessMoves, Articles, Calendar, Directory, Publicity, Reference, Archive, Grading, Products*

Pricecheck: *Annual membership £35.00, National Grading List £15.00, Fritz 5.32 £42.49*

Following an extensive revamp with the arrival of GM John Emms as webmaster and Syringa Turvey as his assistant (ably guided by editor-in-chief and webmaster extraordinaire John Saunders of *British Chess Magazine*), the BCF site now looks quite impressive. The layout has improved immeasurably, making the site easy and convenient to navigate. The content is also very good, comprising all the important information about the BCF as well as lively articles and a useful calendar of events. The BCF's newsletter, *ChessMoves*, which used to be available only in hard copy by subscription, is now accessible to all on the Internet and includes a downloadable database of more than 1,800 games. Analytical articles by Chris Baker and book reviews by Richard Palliser, Gary Lane et al, add value to the site and make it worth a visit even if you are based outside the UK. Grading information is on its way, the site promises.

3) The Campbell Report *****
correspondencechess.com/campbell/index.htm

Headers: *Columns & Articles, Crosstables, News & Reviews, Special Features*

Part of the empire of 'The Correspondence Chess Place' (see review in chapter 9), The Campbell Report is lovingly tended by J. Franklin Campbell, an American correspondence chess (CC) fanatic who avidly reports on all the major CC events, providing easy-to-read crosstables and games to download, as well as entertaining articles by various writers on both CC and over-the-board chess. High-level CC games can be watched here 'live', which in fact means that the position on the board in each game is presented and presumably updated every couple of days, whenever someone makes a move—don't stay logged on while you await the dramatic dénouements!

One of the most unusual reviews posted here is devoted to the magazine, *Chess Pride*, which, believe it or not, is a specialist publication for gay and lesbian chess players. "The goal of raising awareness of the chess accomplishments in the gay/lesbian community is a worthy one, in my opinion," Franklin Campbell writes. "Like any minority, especially one that has traditionally been so suppressed, the accomplishments of members of that minority are often invisible and the absence of successful role models for the members of that minority creates a real and damaging void. Bravo to those who attempt to correct this terrible situation!... The recognition of self-value is of tremendous importance. Chess accomplishment is one measure of accomplishment."

The prolific Franklin Campbell also reviews books and magazines with rather more relevance to correspondence chess and keeps a log on the site of all the changes he makes to it (e.g. 16 March, 2000—added 'A Tribute to our Two American Deans of Chess: Walter G. Muir & George Koltanowski' by Gary Good, to "*On the Square*". 10 March, 2000—added January-February 2000 'The Campbell Report' APCT print column to archive. 8 March, 2000—reached 40,000 hits). To see the big man in the flesh, click on the link to 'Santa Claus Page', where he poses as Santa to proffer his best wishes for the holiday season. Quite a character and quite a site.

4) ChessDate ***
www.freespeech.org/chessdate/index.html
Headers: *News, Events, Kings, Giants, Lessons*

No, it's not a lonely hearts service for chess players who have been spending too long on the Internet—ChessDate is actually a news and historical site in English and Russian. The English spelling is a little dodgy—for instance, when the unfortunate Nikolay Grigoriev is described as an "analist". But apart from that, the content isn't bad, featuring brief reports and crosstables from recent international events and profiles of famous players of the past. Visitors can vote in polls on such pressing matters as 'What is Chess?' (a sport, a science, a game or all of them?) and 'Who is the Best Chess Player in History?'

5) Chess Ireland ***
ireland/iol.ie/~jhurley
Headers: *Results BBS, Games, Email directory, Clubs/contacts, Results, Calendar, Archive, Ratings*

"I too am joining the Internet gold rush," says webmaster John Hurley with typical Irish irony. "Before I go on a roadshow courting interest from the institutions, I have a special offer for all readers. A five per cent equity stake in Chess Ireland can be had by anybody willing to pay my March VISA bill. Contact the editor and get in on the ground floor."

More such humour would be welcome on this site, which is generally very plain in terms of design and writing style, but on the other hand packed with information about Irish chess. It gives names, addresses, telephone numbers, dates, results and links to practically every Irish chess website in existence. There is also an extensive archive of Irish games here to download. Some graphics wouldn't go amiss, though.

6) Chess Sector (Ukrainian Chess Online) ***
chess-sector.odessa.ua
Headers: *Main News, Odessa, Ukraine, World, Games, School, UkrBase, What's New*

GM Mikhail Golubev is the man responsible for the most comprehensive Ukrainian chess resource on the Internet, published in English and Russian, and including news, results and a games database. The site also hosts the homepage of the teenager who was at one stage the world's youngest grandmaster, Ruslan Ponomariov. Golubev himself offers coaching by e-mail, but doesn't say how much he charges. Although Chess Sector provides a useful service for anyone interested in Ukrainian chess, it could do with an imaginative designer and some more entertaining content to offset the bare facts, otherwise the casual surfer won't stay long.

7) Irish Chess Online **
homepage.tinet.ie/~acad

Headers: *Addresses, Chess Diary, Bulletin Board, Events, Clubs, Offical Documents, Ratings*

For some reason this formerly entertaining site has reduced its content and now provides facts and information, but no annotated games or columns, despite having a heavyweight sponsor: the Bank of Ireland. Here on the official website of the ICU (Irish Chess Union) results of Irish tournaments are posted along with the undoubtedly fascinating Bye Laws of the ICU. "Copyright on artwork on this site belongs to JEM Creations," visitors are warned—but where is the artwork? A lacklustre design without any graphics fails to spice up items such a press release from Limerick Chess Club about its forthcoming fundraising events or details of how to enter the Castle Malbork Cup, worthy as these contributions may be.

8) Official Website of the World Chess Federation (FIDE) ****
www.worldfide.com

Headers: *Chess Review, Press Releases, FIDE HandBook, FIDE Officers, FIDE Zones, Commissions, International Arbiters, Title applications, Ratings, Calendar, Honorary Members, About FIDE, Game Zone, FIDE Mail, Get to Know Us, Site Map*

Considering that FIDE is in complete disarray at the time of writing, this is a surprisingly impressive effort. As usual with anything run by FIDE and Kalmyk President (His Excellency) Kirsan Ilyumzhinov, all the hype conveniently glosses over uncomfortable truths: for instance that there are now four people claiming the title of world champion (Garry Kasparov, Anatoly Karpov, Alexander Khalifman and Bobby Fischer) and that the international rating system has collapsed, partly as a result of widespread cheating in Burma. So take what you read on this site with an oversized pinch of salt. The ambitious plans of Ilyumzhinov and fellow Russian businessman, Artiom Tarasov, to turn the whole of world chess into a business under the auspices of FIDE Commerce, have been greeted with concern and scepticism by professional players. This is the place to come to find out exactly what FIDE Commerce proposes to do, as presented in the Memorandum on the Commercialisation of FIDE.

Having read that, if you still doubt the extent of the megalomania behind FIDE, check out the hilarious "Proposed List of Nominees for Enrolment into the FIDE Golden Book on the Occasion of the 75th Anniversary of FIDE". This

125-person list includes French President, Jacques Chirac (No. 1, presumably because the 75th anniversary celebrations were held in Paris); Pope John-Paul II; ex-Soviet President Mikhail Gorbachev; Serge Sarkissian (ex-Armenian national security minister); Henry Kissinger; former British PMs, James Callaghan and Margaret Thatcher; Hollywood stars, Arnold Schwarzenneger and Will Smith; former Wimbledon champion, Boris Becker; numerous minor FIDE officials; and a handful of well-known chess players, including, apparently randomly, Andor Lilienthal and Rafael Vaganian.

Unintended humour aside, there is a wealth of useful information on this site and the design is lively, with plenty of photographs. FIDE's biggest recent events, the Las Vegas world championship and the Batumi European team championship, were covered live on their own spin-off sites and included detailed round-by-round results and information about the players and venues. The entire FIDE rating list, with all its eccentricities, can be downloaded from the site, and players or organisers wishing to check on the status of title applications can also do so here. Crosstables from recent FIDE-approved tournaments from around the world are published on the site, as are FIDE's official rules. On the interactive side, it is already possible to set up your own free FIDE e-mail address, and the Game Zone, where visitors will be able to play each other, is in the process of being tested.

9) Russian Chess ***
www.ruschess.com

Headers: GML, School, Java, Archive, Rusbase, Calendar, Store, Ratings

Pricecheck: Mikhail Tal, A Study in Creativity 1968-1975 (Russian language) US$17.00 inc. transport, Shahcom Electronic Chessboard US$250.00 excl. transport

Changes to the layout of this site haven't added any significant value to it. If anything, it is even more of a mess than before. Visitors are greeted with the inspirational words of Garry Kasparov... "Shahcom has some very good systems". This enigmatic phrase is explained by the fact that Shahcom is the site's sponsor, and if you want to know more about its systems, go to the Store, where you can read all about Shahcom's Electronic Chessboard and Computer Chess Encyclopaedia, although delivery time for the former is 4-8 weeks from the date of order. The site's homepage is an unappealing list of players and their standings in various Russian tournaments. GML (GM Laboratory) is a selection of games with small diagrams annotated very sparsely by GMs Konstantin Sakaev, Sergey Ivanov and Mark Taimanov. In any case, who is going to be interested in Sakaev-Ibragimov, Ivanov-Solovjov or Fedorov-Gulko? Not exactly late

20th-century masterpieces. Photographs are usually a pleasant addition to a website, but in this case the pics of Peter Svidler, Konstantin Sakaev, Sergey Ivanov, Konstantin Aseev and Sergey Ionov are hardly flattering. The site has both Russian and English versions, but the translating is definitely on the ropey side—one of Taimanov's notes reads, "Partners begin with a well developed variation of the Reti opening, where dynamical resources of both sides are not high, due to early relaxation at the center."

In the School, Russian masters and grandmasters are supposedly ready to analyse the games you have played and the positions you are interested in, but the only games available are Svidler-Anand and Kasparov-Topalov, annotated by Sergey Ivanov. Presumably none of the four participants in those games wrote in with a request for Ivanov to analyse their work. The site's resident 'teachers' appear to be hoping that prospective pupils will contact them by e-mail and make a private agreement. Rusbase is only really the beginnings of a database, containing the results and games zipped in PGN, of most world championship matches up to 1986, some candidates' matches, three interzonals, one European team championship (Moscow, 1977), and one USSR championship (the 9th, Leningrad, 1934). The Calendar gives a rough idea of the year's forthcoming events in Russia, but being Russia, they are not all confirmed.

10) Sam Sloan's Chess Page *****
www.shamema.com/chess.htm

Headers: *none (articles grouped by subject)*

The Matt Drudge of chess ought to carry a warning on his site that absolutely no concessions are made to good taste or objectivity. 'Chess Page' is a misnomer, as this sprawling enterprise requires 16 pages simply to list all the articles and photographs contained in it. And if you do manage to read every chess article, Sam Sloan's Homepage (*www.shamema.com*) is a massive collection of juicy news from the US, with thousands of bytes devoted to Monica Lewinsky.

Sam Sloan has strong opinions on certain subjects, such as the goings-on in the US Chess Federation (see 'Why Sam Sloan should be elected to the USCF Executive Board', 'Tom Dorsch and the Law of Libel' and 'Ethics Report is an Outrage') and the FIDE president ('Kirsan Ilyumzhinov, my dear friend, announces that he is a Candidate for Presidency of Russia').

Sloan has also collected an extensive range of documents relating to the proposed commercialisation of FIDE, including responses from American GM Yasser Seirawan and the British Chess Federation. He sometimes writes genuine heartfelt obituaries, of 96-year-old chess journalist George

Koltanowski, for example; and he has an unhealthy interest in the love life of Judit Polgar and bizarre events like the 'Cybersex Chess Torture Trial'. Sloan goes boldly where other journalists fear to tread, clearly not worried about being sued for libel or breach of copyright (he often reproduces articles from the mainstream media on subjects he is interested in).

11) Scottish Chess Association **
www.users.globalnet.co.uk/~sca/sca.htm
Headers: *none (latest postings listed chronologically)*

This disorganised, dull site doesn't really do justice to the Scottish chess scene. It is clear that there is plenty of chess activity in Scotland, but all the site's visitors get are uninspired event reports along the lines of, "Transport difficulties meant that Daniel McGowan was unable to travel with the rest of the squad, his original flight from Tiree being cancelled and the flight the following day on a substitute plane was over five hours late in arriving at Glasgow Airport." An April Fool's Day dig at the Welsh wasn't a bad effort, though, claiming that Councillor Ffion Shetto had called for a ban on chess in schools due to its sexist and racist nature—the queen is expected to do most of the work, there is only one female piece out of 16, and the white pieces always start and usually win.

12) ShakkiNet **
www.shakki.net
Headers: *Info, News, Tournaments, Federations, Clubs*

A minimalist site with neat print set against the background of the white and blue Finnish flag. This style would be more appropriate for a corporate website—it fails to convey the fun side of chess in Finland, if there is one. Many of the pages are in English, but some are only available in Finnish. This isn't really a drawback in most cases, because all that is offered are lists of players and teams and their results in various events. There is also a page of Finnish chess clubs with links to their contact details.

13) TWIC (The Week in Chess) *****
www.chesscenter.com/twic/twicintro.htm
Headers: *Last issue, TWIC TV, Book Reviews by John Watson, PAST TWIC ISSUES (needs registration)*

TWIC reports on every major international chess event, providing crosstables, thousands of games to download, and now TWIC TV, which brings interviews with famous players direct to your computer screen. Everything which has been accumulated on TWIC since its inception is available in the archive. It is also possible to purchase a TWIC CD to avoid lengthy downloading.

TWIC's design is simple and convenient, with relevant links to tournament sites and interesting documents or photographs included at the end of each report. The industrious TWIC webmaster is Mark Crowther, while Malcolm Pein and John Henderson of the London Chess Centre, which sponsors the site, are among its leading contributors. John Watson's regular book reviews are thorough and unbiased.

14) US Chess Online *****
www.uschess.org

Headers: *What's New, Join, Shop, News, Members Only, Ratings, Tournaments, Top Players, Clubs, Scholastics, Correspondence Chess, Governance*

Pricecheck: *Annual membership US$40.00, Fritz 6.0 $49.50/$47.00 (members), Chess Towel Set $35.00/$29.95 (members)*

Visitors to the US Chess Federation's official site are greeted with the words, "This website is very large (over 10,000 pages!). To help you navigate through the website, we suggest you spend a moment and read the 'section descriptions'." Once you've found your way around, you'll notice that the best areas of the site (and the product discounts) are reserved for USCF members. The Members Only Area features audio lectures and Java lessons, post-coverage of elite tournaments such as Linares with GM commentaries and games on Java boards, readers' games and chess columns. Non-members can purchase a one-day pass to this section for US$5.00.

A relatively new section in this site—accessible to non-members—is the Correspondence Chess section, where you can check out CC rules and columns, and enter a "wide variety of rated correspondence chess events, two of which involve awarding the title of USCF's Absolute CC Champion and USCF's Golden Knights Open Champion each year". There are entry fees, however. The US Chess Online shop has an extensive range of products, which is hardly surprising on such a commercialised site. Expect to see its shares floated on the stock market in the not-too-distant future...

15) Welsh Chess Homepage **
www.users.globalnet.co.uk/~pbevan/index.htm

Headers: *Officers, Poll, Calendar, News, Grading List, AGM, Gallery, Games, Problem, WCU Fees, Constitution, Chat, Entry Forms*

This is the sloppily-designed official site of the Welsh Chess Union, its main attraction being a rousing rendition of the Welsh National Anthem. Flashing icons overlap on each other and lead only to boring pages of text. Welsh chess players can, however, check their grades and find out basic information about events in Wales. Visitors will also learn that the WCU's motto is 'Ymsodiad dewr; Amddiffyniad sicr' ('Bold in attack; Secure in defence')—but they won't find out how to pronounce it.

As the site only seems to be updated every few months, items such as 'Report on the recent 4NCL weekend', or 'Report on the recent South Wales Masters' are unlikely to provide up-to-the-minute news or results. Nor are they accompanied by diagrams, so it is hardly enlightening to learn that "Richard Jones... captured a Knight for three pawns and quickly laid waste Rudd's king side. Rudd's connected, passed pawns never got moving and instead it was Jones on the verge of promoting a pawn and winning a further bishop, who provoked a resignation from his West Country rival." Objectivity is also somewhat lacking, considering that the above account was written by Richard Jones himself. The problem page features a ridiculously difficult mate in five from the game Weissegerber-Rellstab (Geneva 1933)—neither of the players involved appear to be Welsh. If you feel the urge to make contact with real, live Welsh chess players, try the chat room.

3
Clubs & Events

Many international chess events have their own website for the duration of play, but the site is neglected afterwards. These are soon out of date, so this chapter includes only those sites which are more or less continuously providing coverage of events. The best of these is the 'Lost Boys Chess Page', an exciting, vibrant site which exploits all the possibilities of multimedia. A large number of chess clubs now boast sites, yet these are often very bland and rarely updated. Some of the better club sites are reviewed here—often because they offer something extra, on top of basic club information, which a wider audience can appreciate.

A/ Webmaster Hall of Fame

Dave Regis, Exeter Chess

Please introduce yourself.

I'm Dave Regis, an East Anglian migrant to the West country and a chess enthusiast. I look after sites for Exeter and Exeter Junior Clubs, for the Devon County Chess Association, and for the West of England Chess Union. The Exeter site is best known for its coaching materials, but there's some lighter stuff in there too: quotes and stories.

My day job is research manager for an independent research unit specialising in schools' health education. What's the overlap with coaching? Education, certainly, and computers, but also an emphasis on being aware of your own development.

How often do you have a chance to play chess?

I play most weeks at the Exeter club, and also a few weekend congresses a year; I also do my bit for club and county. It comes to 30 or so competitive games a year, which leaves me constantly feeling out of practice. I suppose we all have a 'chance' to play at any time of day on the Internet, but I have to wait my turn at the PC behind the missus and her daughter, and chess has to take its turn behind the house and garden.

When and why did you decide to create a website?

The expansion of the Internet in the early nineties coincided with a request to develop both a junior club in Exeter and a programme of coaching for the senior club. So I was looking for coaching ideas, and hoped that, to coin a phrase from across the herring pond, what goes around, comes around. I knew that there were some games and examples that I found very instructive, and I hoped by telling people about my favourites, they would do the same. I was also excited about the Internet in general when I first came across it, as a means for people to share information. In that respect, my inspiration has been people like the Free Software Foundation and the folks at the GNU project.

How easy is the site to maintain and have you experienced any serious technical problems with it?

The big technical hurdle I had to overcome at the outset was creating diagrams automatically, which was solved for me in 1994 by Andy Duplain. He kindly added a widget to his CBASCII utility, and the rest was handled by some Unix tools. Nowadays I think the latest ChessBase comes with a web page facility, but back then it was all home cooking, and lots of greedy downloading from the Pittsburgh Archive. Since then, it's been fairly straightforward, because I don't go in for any fancy design features. Although every time the operating system gets upgraded I have a little series of headaches, and I think it's actually less efficient now than before the operating system was 'improved'. (Computers are like that.)

Where do you get your material from and does anybody else help with the site?

The site started as a record of our coaching sessions, where we hope to pull ourselves up by our collective bootstraps. So everyone who has taken part in that group has helped. I have badgered people at the club over the years to give little presentations on their own games and ideas, and to suggest topics for me to research, and so there's a constant fund of material there. Ken Hills, Peter Lane, Agust Karlsson and Tony Dempsey have particularly distinguished themselves. From my end, I've got a big library and a good memory, so a lot comes from my own reading. And the readers of the site help a lot with clarifying and correcting. But the real origin of the material is the ongoing debate about the question we keep asking on club nights, "why aren't we better at chess?"

What material can people find on your site that is not available in books or magazines?

I think the chess is the same but the commentary is different; I also like to include a lot of annotated amateur games. It's determinedly for the club player by the club player. You do get a lot from listening to classy players talk about chess, but you get something else from listening to amateurs chew over a position—people who aren't necessarily that good at chess, but who are serious and reflective, talking about what they find helpful. They may have recently passed the point you are at, perhaps after a struggle, and may be more able to offer an insight than someone who beat their first GM in their teens.

Also, we've done some of the sifting for you. There are some classic isolated queen's pawn examples that are lazily repeated from book to book, and we should have them (or something like them) on our site.

Why is coaching and providing coaching resources on your site so important to you?

Four reasons. Firstly, my own desire to improve—your understanding of something improves drastically when you have to explain it to someone else. Secondly, as a record of our struggle to understand and address the problems of our own improvement, and to share these with other people who are going through the same thing. Thirdly, people were so kind to me when I was learning, that I'd like to put a bit back. And lastly, the more there is for free, the harder I hope the book publishers will have to try. I think a lot of published books are pretty sloppy, and I really resent lashing out £15 for something I think I could have written myself! (I have written a book myself, so people can say the same about me.)

Would you say that Exeter Chess Club has gained through having a page on your site?

Well, it's obviously given it a higher profile—foreign visitors often know about us through the site—but you can't weigh your profile. Concretely, we have got some nice free coaching games and ideas, we have made some links with clubs in the UK and abroad that we have played matches against over the Internet, and it's increasingly often a first point of contact for new members. Also, when we were putting together our Centenary book, I picked up a couple of contributions from ex-members who got in touch over the net.

Have you enjoyed providing a website and do you receive much feedback?

I've found it very satisfying. Three of my passions in life have been chess, computers and the capacity for ordinary people to improve their lot through collective endeavour—and the website tickles all three.

I get a modest stream of bouquets and brickbats by e-mail, most of which I enjoy hugely. The biggest pleasure is hearing from club players who reckon it's improved their game, although of course it's very flattering to get praise from stronger players. Even some of the criticism is very constructive: one character complained the site was a bit difficult to navigate—there are hundreds of documents there —but also helpfully enclosed an index!

Other favourite e-mails include the one I got when I asked for a copy of a game Petrosian-Peters from Lone Pine, and got a note from a player who actually watched the game, and could describe poor Jack Peters' puzzled expression—it really brought the score to life! Another one I remember was when I was putting together a piece on castling, and was looking for a real-life example of the trap ...♖xb2?, 0-0-0+. Mickey Adams then sprung this on Dreev about a fortnight later, and along with the score, I got an amusing e-mail from Matt Guthrie accusing me of arranging the whole thing with Mickey, probably over a pint in a pub overlooking the River Tamar on the Devon-Cornwall border.

What future plans do you have for the site?

I'm comfy with the basics, or at least I'm confident I know what's wrong with them. I'd certainly like to have more contributions that don't have my name on them, so anyone out there with an instructive game or experience is welcome to get in touch. I often think about including more book reviews, just to vent a bit of spleen really, but I never get around to it and there are in any event lots of good review sites around (John Watson, Randy Bauer and Tim Harding stand out).

A more useful plan is to develop more content around one of my hobby horses, chess psychology. I believe the chess thinking of amateurs is often interestingly different to that of masters and if we knew more about that, we'd probably understand a lot more about the barriers to our improvement. And I'd like to extend the range of levels that the site caters for—upwards and downwards.

Do you play chess on the Internet and if so, where? Do you think that Internet chess clubs will eventually supplant normal chess clubs?

I won't play at ICC as I regret the way it was hijacked; I have an account on most of the Free Internet Chess Servers and have played most often at the American and German sites. I still like 'real' chess—a local weekender provides many pleasures that the isolated Internet experience cannot—a chance to catch up with the local characters, browse a bookstall, cheer on the juniors, tease the controllers. Even if Internet chess got rid of lag, lag-flaggers, computer cheaters and disconnecters, I wouldn't expect it to replace face-to-face chess.

Which websites are your favourites, and which do you consider to be rivals?

The nice thing for amateurs like me with sites on the Internet is that there are only friends, and no rivals. In terms of other free coaching sites, there are some good materials at ChessWise University, the UMBC Master Preparation course, and at DiaPlaza. And Tryfon at Barnet has got another good co-operative development project going, mostly 'white papers' about the openings.

I've got a lot of time for BritBase—both as an important archive but also as a source of more amateur games. To be honest, I don't get a lot out of studying the latest GM encounter in the Grophulous Variation of the Lirpaloff Defence. I'd sooner look at something a bit more accessible and John's tournaments have got a lot of interesting sub-master games.

For the rest, I think the best index still currently active is Chessopolis. Although Yahoo! has obviously got a lot of material, I always find the links are too many mouse clicks away for comfort. (I take my hat off to anyone who commits to maintaining an index: sites are up and down like prices at Christmas!)

Another great one-stop shop is Palamede—a group of important free European chess sites with different specialities (pictures, publishing, news, variants, etc.). The Chess Café is always worth a visit, they've really got some cracking columnists there. And I like the Correspondence chess site a lot, more good columnists. And ChessMail. In fact, I don't have time to keep up with developments in all the sites I like.

B/ Best of the Web

Film of War

The sun beats down on Oxford Street... August 1994...
England's Greed and Peasant shopping Land ...At the Virgin
Mega Store you veer right. Over the zebra crossings... past
the Kentucky Fried Chicken... round the Bureau De Change...
into the hotel and down to the 'production box'. You are in
5-star air-conditioned comfort. You are at the very last Lloyds
Bank Chess Masters.

ONE WAVE OF YOUR UB40 AND YOU'RE IN!

Three quid saved. Breezing past the 'lower orders' on the
bottom boards who are technically, comparatively, on paper
and by every other measuring device devised by mankind—
better than you. However... today you stand apart from this rat
race. You are a spectator, above it all, an observer, an
extra-systemic intergalactic star trooper, bored with beating
Mr Spock at 3-Dimensional Chess. And you're headed
straight for those very special top four boards. Special
because the games are mirrored high above on huge hi-tech
demonstration boards. The ultimate goal for the lesser
players... but oh, what a bittersweet triumph! Swindles and
brilliancies that would dazzle in the local league are blown up
to cinematic size. Into a vast 'Film of War'... and the heat is
on... there is no room for error. The screenplay has the
pretender getting killed in the final reel. There is five hours to
complete the rewrite. The King must die!

You sit down to watch them begin their efforts. You are not
really a 3D GM but a BCF 148. Aha! but no one here knows
that... how could they? You are dressed the same as a
grandmaster—scruffy. Keep your mouth shut and look
intelligent. You're the only one who knows that you can only
spot the really big stars by their occasionally wet hair. Their
wet hair? Yes, witness the Russian GM sitting imperiously on
Board 1... it proves beyond doubt that he has just descended
down the 5-star stairs from his 5-star breakfast and... 5-star
shower. His opponent has bussed it over from the YMCA.

And now how about a look around the other boards that
grace this vast arena? You stroll, as a King would, smiling
enigmatically. You descend on an interesting little game and
instantly assess it. White is about to win with a rather amusing
little brilliancy. You smile at a watching GM. Two chess brains
as one in this ship of fools. Generous in your silent praise
despite your unjust place in the club's 5th team. Two moves
later White has lost, but there's no time for detail.

After four hours of fascination, you look up and see the
people representing the other side of the chess coin. An
all-too recognisable sub-strata of this community. No need to
feel inferior now... In come the SUITS. Sad, forlorn figures

clutching briefcases and wistfully watching a game they could no doubt excel in if only they had all day to waste studying. And there's no place to hide for the SUITS. It's obvious to one and all that they've dropped in after a day's work. Part-timers! They secretly wonder whether this community of pure thought and alcohol couldn't be doing something useful. Meanwhile their cobweb covered brains creak happily back to life.

You look back at the top boards. If only you could capture the magic and use it at your club's next league game. Shirov, to move, is gazing into space, dreaming up deadly combinations... Norwood is a deadly surprise combination of designer clothes and grandmaster strength... Dr Nunn is resplendent in white, sipping from a can of Coca-Cola produced in a factory in America 1000 times smaller than his brain. You'll play your next few games in your best clothes, sipping coke and staring out into space... and lose just the same.

So enjoy, one and all... GMs, IMs, FMs, Suits, Spacemen, YMCAs... Cadogan Club Masters... it's the final Lloyds Bank. A sporting event where you walk next to the Gods. It's like being allowed on to the pitch next to Ryan Giggs to watch him take a free kick for Manchester United... shaking your head in despair if he miscues.

And so to the finale. The last prizegiving reaches its climax but the final winner, a 17-year-old absent-minded genius from Russia, isn't here. David Norwood gives a speech instead and says that the winner was last spotted wandering across the green and pleasant grass of Hyde Park. It is, perhaps, an easy mistake to make for someone with limited English, and family and trainer waiting in a hotel across the park. You also suspect that the money and fame came a very poor second as the sun sets on the wondrous Lloyds Bank Chess Masters.

Graham Brown
King's Head Chess Club (www.khcc.org.uk/fow.htm)

C/ Websites

1) Edinburgh Chess Club ***
www.jthin.co.uk/ecc.htm

Headers: *History, Club News, Calendar, Membership, Open Events*

Founded in 1822, Edinburgh is one of the oldest chess clubs in the world, and it was one of the first British clubs to set up a website. This portrays Edinburgh as a lively club with a number of talented youngsters, including Women's Amateur World Champion, Elaine Rutherford. Many games are available but not all can be downloaded, whilst the overall appearance is a little bland. There is, however, much useful information about the club and a heartfelt tribute by webmaster Bill Marshall to his favourite player, Mikhail Tal.

2) Exeter Chess *****
www.ex.ac.uk/~dregis/DR/chess.html

Headers: *Me, Exeter CC, Coaching, Canon, Books, Quotes*

Any prospective coach would do well to check out all Dave Regis' information on the matter before giving any tuition. Regis may only be around 1900 strength but he is an experienced coach and has assisted in weekly forums at the Exeter Chess Club. Many games can be downloaded to illustrate various points, including tactical patterns and clock control, whilst there are several sample handouts available as well as an excellent selection of links to other sites dealing with coaching.

Regis' book recommendations are also impressive, and he believes that you must learn descriptive notation to read the great works, whilst he also uses his own games and hundreds of chess-related quotes to make several points relevant to helping a player improve. This enjoyable and informative site is also the home of Exeter Chess Club.

3) First Saturday ***
www.elender.hu/~firstsat

Headers: *International grandmaster tournament, International master tournament, FIDE-master-tournament, Program for year 2000, Time and venue, Useful advices about the city Budapest, Accommodation in Budapest 2000, Coming to the FIRST SATURDAY tournament (application form)*

Pricecheck: *GM tournament entry ELO/DM: below 2301/450, 2301-2350/400, 2351-2400/350, above 2400/300*

Ebullient chess organiser Laszlo Nagy (his surname appropriately means 'big') runs tournaments in Budapest starting on the first Saturday of each month for stronger players looking to gain rating points or norms. This site provides all the information needed to enter a First Saturday tournament along with links to other sites where results and games of previous tournaments can be found. Helpful advice is also given about Budapest, such as where the best baths and Chinese restaurants are, whilst there is a range of accommodation on offer, from three-star hotels to rooms with local families.

4) 4NCL ***
freespace.virgin.net/nigel.chess96/4ncl/4n-m-idx.htm

Headers: *Results 99/00, Dates & Venue, Fixtures Division 1, Fixtures Division 2, Team Information, Management Board, Competition Rules, Officials, Guidance on Transfers*

In the space of a very few years, the 4NCL (Four Nations' Chess League) has become the British equivalent of the prestigious German Bundesliga, attracting the cream of British chess, hundreds of strong regional players, and many famous names from abroad, such as Mikhail Gurevich and Alexander Morozevich. Since John Saunders, who ran the original 4NCL site very well, took over at BCM, the 4NCL has created a new website, run by Nigel Johnson, the 4NCL's Events Director. Here, fixtures for the forthcoming season are posted, whilst players and spectators can also easily find out a bit about each team along with all the official rules of the competition. For the latest 4NCL news and game downloads, however, you will now find these incorporated into the BCM website's News section, although they may reappear on this site soon.

5) Greater Grace Christian Academy Chess! **
www.nf3.com/ggchess/default.htm

Headers: *Upcoming Events!, 1999 State Champs!, About GGCA., Subscribe to GGCA Chess Newsletter!*

The GGCA of Baltimore, Maryland, offers "a well-rounded K-12 curriculum in Academics, Athletics, and Biblical Studies". Thus it is little surprise that their chess club's website combines chess with Christ, and webmaster Jon Saboe has even set up a discussion forum on the subject (to subscribe write to *christ-chess-subscribe@egroups.com*). Most of us feel like praying occasionally during a game, but GGCA makes it compulsory.

A role model is St Teresa of Avila, "an outstanding chess player who authored a famous treatise on spirituality entitled *The Way of Perfection.* She devoted one chapter on how to develop one's ability to receive God's love, and used chess piece development as an analogy." Other anecdotes, and not all with a religious connection, also provide much interest and should impress your chess-playing friends. The other entertaining aspect of this site is the club member biographies, although the appeal soon wears off unless you are actually a pupil or teacher at the Academy. Kids are asked, "What is your favorite chess plan or strategy?", "What is your favorite Bible verse?" and "Do you have any prayer requests?", whilst Joseph Haroun prays "that we can have a chess team as large or larger than Cockeysville".

6) Hull Chess Club ****
www.hullchessclub.karoo.net

Headers: *Book Reviews, Opening Theory, Members' Games*

Many chess clubs would do well to make their site as clear and well-organised as this, Jim Hawksley's. The site is regularly updated and it contains just the right amount of information for prospective members. The split screen layout makes the site all the easier to navigate and there are a number of impressive little gimmicks. The homepage features headlines, with links to the articles they represent, which rather confirm the site's claim of being 'Yorkshire's Premier Club', as well as hyperlinks to the latest five books reviews. There are good links to most of the best chess sites on the web, whilst Hawksley, who is quite a good amateur theoretician, presents a very interesting Sveshnikov novelty, under opening theory, which has even caught the attention of Alexei Shirov! The selection of members' game is still rather small, although these games can easily be played through on a JavaScript board and some feature fairly good annotations. All the latest publications by Batsford, Everyman and Gambit are reviewed, but as the book review page grows, it could probably do with a search engine and a slightly less bland layout.

7) Kilkenny Chess Club ***
ireland.iol.ie/~mbuckley

Headers: *In the beginning there was Spassky..., Can I bring my boyfriend?, Win a prize, Compose a Chess Limerick!, Private—For Eyes of British Chess Champion Only, Not all Gentlemen are Gentlemen!!, Not your ordinary Committee!, We have a problem, or two, At the court of King Boris, Almost chess, almost, James Mason, one of our own, The Heidenfeld Heroes Picture 167Kb*

The club that hosts Ireland's biggest congress is also home to the country's most jovial chess organisers.

According to their article, 'What a Committee!', ten years after the club was founded in 1970, a subcommittee recommended two levels of membership: "Level one membership costing £500 per annum. This entitles the member to: castigate, vilify, insult, slander, libel and question the parentage of anyone on the club committee... Level two membership costing £10 per annum. This entitles the member to become a slave of the club, he must work on its behalf like he's supposed to work when at work! He must love it like he's supposed to love his wife and must treat and nurture it at every opportunity like his own flesh and blood. Kilkenny chess club fortunately has many of the latter type of member, whilst 'enjoying' none of the former."

Boris Spassky found the charms of the Kilkenny committee irresistible and came to visit Ireland at the club's request. The story is related here in, 'In the beginning there was Spassky...' and 'At the court of King Boris'. Several of the articles on the site have appeared in the British magazine *CHESS*, including the superbly researched article revealing the real name of

Irish chess hero, James Mason, by Jim Hayes. Alongside the articles there are a limerick competition and a couple of weird chess problems involving cats. Sadly, despite Jack Lowry's Kilkenny Congress becoming even stronger every year, only the games from the 1996 congress can be downloaded, whilst there are not even results from the more recent events. The articles provided here are enjoyable and often humorous, but the site really does need updating much more often.

8) King's Head Chess Club *****
www.khcc.org.uk/start.shtml

Headers: *Information, Puzzles, Games, Articles*

An enjoyable site which certainly appears to confirm King's Head's claim that it is "London's most exciting and friendly, central pub-based chess club". A large number of members have submitted articles, games and problems, whilst there is plenty of information for prospective members. The game annotations of FM Steve Berry and guest contributor GM Bogdan Lalic are very good, and many games can be easily played through online. There is also a humorous and useful guide to French for chess players by Alex Bourke, author of *Vegetarian London*, whilst the articles on all the club's foreign excursions are enjoyable and well worth reading, as indeed are most of the articles available.

9) Lost Boys Chess Page *****
www.lostcity.nl/chess/ccs/defaultnl2.htm

Headers: *Game Base, Tournaments*

For news, results and live games from the biggest Dutch and international tournaments, such as Wijk aan Zee, the Frankfurt Chess Classic, and the Dutch Championship, this is one of the best places to go. Flashy, hi-tech presentation heightens the atmosphere of events so that you can experience some of the tension without leaving your armchair. Coverage often includes game annotations, player and tournament information, and cartoons by José Diaz. The Game Base allows searches under a number of categories, and then the games can either be viewed online, with diagrams, or e-mailed to you in PGN format.

10) MontiChess ***
www.chuh.org/Monticello/Chess/default.htm

Headers: *ESA, ESSCL, Problems, EndGames, Features, NorthCoastScene*

This site belongs to Monticello chess club in Cleveland Heights, Ohio. Most Fridays they host a 30-minute tournament, and full details about these events are provided. There are also interesting weekly problems, which you can solve and then appear on the winners' roll of honour. Endgames are also featured, and there is a good range of links to sites with areas devoted to endings, whilst you can also view a few annotated games. These are dubbed 'Full Length Feature Presentations' and include a Ruy Lopez with notes by IM Calvin Blocker. General information about the strong chess scene in Cleveland, whose Main Library houses the John G. White collection, comprising nearly 40,000 volumes of historical chess material, also provides some interesting reading and links.

11) Northgate Chess Club ***
members.xoom.com/chekmate111

Headers: *Beginning, Openings, Middlegame, Endgame, Tactics, Strategy, Analyzing, Deciding, Defense, Practice, Study, Info, ECO, History, Champs, Books, My Games*

Tim Eberly, a strong club player and experienced coach from Seattle, offers some excellent tutorial material on all aspects of the game. The ambitious section on openings, includes an explanation of the Ruy Lopez, the Falkbeer Counter Gambit and the Two Knights' Defence; whilst for beginners, Eberly explains the main ideas behind the French Defence for Black. Eberly's explanations are thorough, clear and aimed mainly at the average club player, although in certain cases more examples and diagrams would not go amiss. The Encyclopaedia of Chess Openings is exactly what it claims to be, listing the main lines of every opening under the sun, although several other sections are still waiting to be completed. All players, from beginner to strong club player, should benefit from visiting this site, which effectively offers a wide range of free tuition alongside the many illustrative famous quotations.

12) Palamede Calendrier *****
www.palamede.com/cgi-bin/calendar/calendar.pl

Headers: *None*

Connected to the large French Palamede site, the Calendrier is well worth a visit even if your French is virtually non-existent. Many websites contain a diary of national events, but none contains such a large international tournament listing as is available here. Searching is by month, and each day of that month lists all the international events taking place that day. Clicking on the day a tournament is due to start brings up all the contact information about that event and other events starting on that day.

4
Where to Play

Playing chess on the Internet is now so popular that even search engines such as Yahoo! are offering their own sites. The only dilemmas are where to play, when there is so much choice, and whether it is worth paying a subscription or using one of the free sites. If you do decide to subscribe to the Internet Chess Club, you'll get more than your money's worth, with the opportunity to watch the world's elite playing live in supertournaments; lectures; simuls; versatile software; and thousands of potential opponents online, 24 hours a day.

The Internet is also the perfect medium for correspondence games, and alongside the new sites, which run e-mail tournaments, the established correspondence chess organisations have also cottoned on to this newfangled technology. Entry to e-mail tournaments is either free or low-cost, but most serious sites require you to play a practice game first with a tutor to ensure that you follow the rules. Remember that if you abandon an e-mail tournament while it is in progress, you could be spoiling things for several other players who have put months of effort into their analysis.

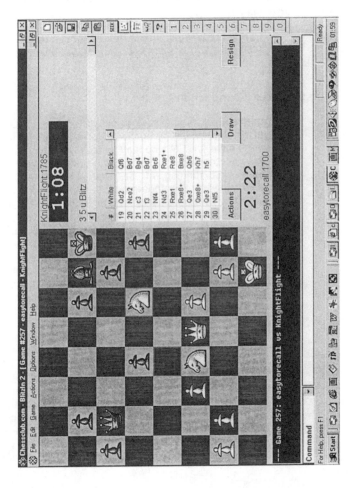

Internet Chess Club (www.chessclub.com)

A/ Webmaster Hall of Fame

Danny Sleator ('darooha'), Internet Chess Club

Please introduce yourself

I'm 46, married, and have a two-year-old child. I'm a professor of Computer Science at Carnegie Mellon University. I work in the areas of natural language processing and data structure design. If you want to know more about my childhood, read *Oddballs*, a book by my brother William Sleator.

How strong a chess player are you, do you play much in general, and do you play on ICC?

I am a pretty weak player (rating about 1500). I do play quite a bit on ICC. I like some of the wild variants (crazyhouse and losers) as much as regular chess.

Who started ICC and when?

In the early '90s, a system called the Internet Chess Server (ICS) was written by some students at various universities. I don't have a list of who they were, where they were, and what they contributed. In 1992 I came upon the site, which at that time was running at Carnegie Mellon, and was being maintained by two undergraduate students (John Chanak and Bill Kish, who were not among the authors of the system).

The system was quite primitive, and very buggy. For example, the code that detected checkmate had a bug that would identify some positions as mate that were not mate. The system could not detect when a game was a dead draw (for example, two lone kings). So people could often be found trying to run their opponent's clock out by running their king around quickly. I decided that I wanted to add a new feature to the system, which was the increment clock system. (This turned out to be called the Fischer clock, which I found out later.) So I got the code from Chanak and started to work on it. Once I had deciphered the code to add increments, it only made sense to start fixing the bugs and add new features.

I continued to do this for about three years. At this point I had rewritten the entire system, and the new parts that I had added were much bigger and more complex than what I had started with. At this point I decided that I either had to turn the ICS into a commercial company, or just give it away for somebody else to maintain. I decided to work with my wife and two others that I met online to turn it into the ICC.

Who developed MrSpock and was it done specially for ICC?

MrSpock was originally developed by Eric Peterson, one of the owners of ICC (who helped in the commercialisation). It's since been rewritten by Bert Enderton, who is an ICC employee who has taken over chess server development.

Why should people pay to play on ICC when they can play elsewhere for free?

Many reasons. For one thing, our service is better than the free servers. It has more features, and is more reliable. I won't bother to list them here. There are administrators to handle adjudications and to find and eliminate cheaters. There is a customer service number you can call for help. By charging, we eliminate the worst and most obnoxious people.

Which site or sites do you see as your main competitors and how do you stay ahead of them?

KasparovChess online is probably our most worrisome competitor. They have a lot of money, and the Kasparov name. They seem to be trying to directly attack our niche. (Although, so far, they have not been as potent as it seems they could have been.) They're trying to buy up the 'broadcast rights' to major chess tournaments, although the exact legal status of such 'rights' is ambiguous.

Fretting about what a competitor is going to do or not do is not a productive way to spend our time. There have been a lot of threats from a lot of different sites from the very beginning. None of them have turned out to be very serious. What we're doing is just continuously making improvements to our service, and making cross-promotional deals with as many sites as we can.

How has the playing format changed since ICC started—what new innovations have there been?

There have been dozens. Here is a short list:

- move timestamping
- history lists
- tomato system
- multiple ratings
- bughouse and other wild games
- improved interfaces
- database of GM games
- increased capacity for simultaneous logins
- multiple servers sharing ratings

Have there been any unsuccessful features that you have dropped?

Not really features... some unsuccessful policies have changed.

How did you attract titled players initially, and what special benefits do they get now?

We did a lot of work to attract GMs. We went to tournaments and gave them little gift bags with BlitzIn disks. We called them on the phone and installed software on their machines. We paid them to play on ICC. We implemented the chekel system that allows them to give lessons and accept payment from other ICC members.

How do you verify that someone really is the titled player they are claiming to be?

They must fax proof of identity.

Which players in the top 100 are the most frequent visitors to ICC?

Probably Topalov, Shirov, Svidler, Short, Kaidanov, Yermolinsky. There are many others. I could look it up but I don't have time this minute. You can look for yourself. Type 'best' on ICC and then type 'help gm-bio' to find out who they are.

Do famous players ever complain that they are bombarded with messages when they play on ICC?

I am not aware of this happening.

Have you had any troublemakers, and if so what do you do about them?

We have a lot of them. We have many mechanisms to deal with them—muzzling, IP filtering, banning.

What was the most popular event hosted by ICC and how many people watched?

The 2nd Deep-Blue vs. Kasparov match was the most popular. About 2,400 people watched.

How do you decide which events to show live?

We show all events that are (1) of interest to our members and (2) we can obtain easily.

Do you pay the players who give lectures and simuls?

Yes.

Do you make a profit when people pay to watch, e.g. Kasparov-Kramnik?

We made no money from Kasparov-Kramnik. All the money went to the organisers. And we don't make any profit from people watching. The benefit is satisfied customers and membership renewals.

Does ICC make a profit or is that not the intention?

Yes, it does make a profit.

What is the biggest complaint from ICC members?

Probably lag, and the desire for more different ratings.

Do you think that ICC has encouraged people to play chess who normally wouldn't bother going out to a club?

Yes, definitely. I have heard a lot of people say that. I'm an example of this.

Would you agree with people who say that playing via the Internet is antisocial?

It's different. It has some advantages and disadvantages. I find it less intimidating not to have to look somebody in the face.

What's new on ICC in the past year?

There have been hundreds of big and small improvements. We introduced new ratings for losers' chess and crazyhouse. We made extensive improvements to the interfaces. We modified the free trial system to let people with free e-mail accounts get free trials. We added a new 'trainingbot' and endgame robots. We've moved to a better Internet provider and bought new server machines. We're planning a bunch of new features and services in the near future.

B/ Best of the Web

Ceremonies of the Horsemen (The Journal of the IECC Rank and File)

PGN NOTATION AND GAME REPORTS BY MICHAEL MCSHANE (1309 USA)

It has recently come to the attention of the IECC that although everyone goes through the New Member Program, sometimes we tend to forget the proper PGN notation. As a Tournament Director (TD, for short) on the Knockout Team who does proofreading and a New Member Guide I feel I can help many of you understand it better. I would like to take a few minutes of your time to review this with you.

Before I begin, I would like to tell you why PGN notation is so important to us. We at the IECC archive all of our games. This means we need to be able to keep a record of the moves, result, what they played in and so forth, not only for the staff but the members as well. Therefore, we have to set a standard notation that we use that isn't too difficult. PGN notation is well known and meets this standard.

Since we archive all our games that means one of the TDs, either me or someone else depending on what type of game you are playing, have to be able to read it, proofread it, and eliminate any unnecessary text. This proofreading means we have to be sure of proper spacing, the header is correct, the result is correct in both places (as I will discuss later), and so forth. This must be done as it is an automated system that does the rating.

I think I can better explain the notation from this point on now that you have a feeling for how it is done. Let me start by going over the header with you. Here is a header from one of my games in the New Member Program. While I am mentioning the New Member Program let me say, ask as many questions as you can at this time! The guides in the program are here to teach you proper notation as well as to familiarize you with the rules. This is your best chance to get any questions you may have out of the way. The more you ask the fewer problems you will have with PGN notation (and the rules). In the Program we believe there is no such thing as a stupid question—only unresolved questions!

[Event "New Member Program"]
This is what the code or the game is called. If you see a decimal point with a number after it the number following the decimal point is the round number. The Tournament Director (TD) will tell you what to put in here. If there is a dash in the event please remember to put it in here.
[Site "IECC"]
This is a constant. Don't change this.
[Date "1998.12.6"]
The TD will assign a date for you.
[Round "1"] The round is always "1" unless the event has a decimal point in it. In this case, the number after the first decimal point is the round. Ignore the numbers after the second decimal point, if there are any.
[White "McShane, Michael"]
Who is White? Note it goes last name then first.
[Black "Kemerling, Ken"]
Who is Black? Note it goes last name then first.

[Result "*"]
This should be an asterisk until you have an outcome. The three outcomes are 1-0 (White wins), 1/2-1/2 (Draw), and 0-1 (Black wins). Do not use decimals when recording a draw (.5-.5). White always sends a copy of the game report, which is the moves of the game with the final result included, to the opponent and the Tournament Director unless Black wins. If Black wins, he sends it.

Please note the generic words (event, site, etc.) are exactly one space away from the specific words, which are in quotation marks. The whole thing is enclosed in square brackets on each individual line. So when you look at this as a header, without the notes I have given you, it will look like this:

[Event "New Member Program"]
[Site "IECC"]
[Date "2000.12.6"]
[Round "1"]
[White "McShane, Michael"]
[Black "Kemerling, Ken"]
[Result "*"]

Next come the moves. There should be exactly one blank line between the header and the first move. Moves are done using standard algebraic notation. I will quickly review this for you, but not in great depth as I am pretty sure you know it.

Piece	Signified by
Pawn	file (a-h) it is on
kNight	N
Bishop	B
Rook	R
Queen	Q
King	K

You will note I miscapitalized the Knight. I did this on purpose for a reason. I wanted to give a way for beginners to remember what the correct notation is for a kNight move.

There are three ways of remembering it. The first is to remember that N and not K is used for its notation. The second also tells you the phonic you hear when you say this word is N, so you should use an N for notation. The last one is a saying I came up with:

The kNight is Noble,
While the King has his Kingdom.

I hope this helps any beginners out here who have difficulty remembering this. Now here are a few notations that are commonly done incorrectly.

Notation	Correct	Wrong
Castles Kingside	O-O (using capital o's)	0-0 (using zeroes)
Castles Queenside	O-O-O (using capital o's)	0-0-0 (using zeroes)
En Passant	exf6 {e.p}	exf6 e.p. or exf6
En Passant Check	exf7+ {e.p.}	exf7+ e.p. or exf7+

The en passant check may also be double check or mate by changing the symbols appropriately. Here are a few more notes on PGN notation.

Type of Move	How To do It In PGN
Moving	Piece notation and square moved to (Nc3)
Capturing	Piece notation, an x, and square moved to (Kxe7)
Check	Move made followed by a plus sign (Nxf6+ or Rf7+)
Checkmate	Move made followed by the number sign (exf6#)
Double Check	Move made followed by two plus signs (Rd3++)

Please note that you use the same notation for both discovered check and check. When you send your games make sure they are in this notation. Also follow the following rules for spacing:

1. There is no space between the move number and White's move.

2. There is exactly one space between the White's move and Black's move.

3. There is exactly one space between the Black's move and the move number.

I have cut out the header to show you an example of how the moves are written.

1.e4 Nf6 2.e5 Nd5 3.d4 d6 4.c4 Nb6 5.Nc3 dxe5 6.dxe5 Qxd1+ 7.Nxd1 e6 8.Nc3 Bb4 * You may be wondering what the asterisk is for. This symbolises who is on move. It may be deleted or a question mark may be used instead.

Please be sure to write in paragraph format and not column format. That is the way our PGN reader reads all the games. Okay, now I have one thing I have to ask everyone. When you send in the header please be sure you have written the event correctly! Otherwise the wrong game may be rated!

Here is a complete game. Please notice that there is no move number after the last move is made, and the result is written both in the header and after the last move made.

[Event "KO-508.1.6"]
[Site "IECC"]
[Date "2000.07.27"]
[Round "1"]
[White "Attardi, Ubaldo"]
[Black "Hakuc, Waclaw"]
[Result "0-1"]
1.d4 d5 2.c4 dxc4 3.e4 b5 4.a4 Bb7 5.d5 c6 6.axb5 cxd5
7.exd5 Qxd5 8.Qg4 Nf6 9.Qf4 Ne4 10.Ra4 e5 11.Qg4 Bb4+
12.Rxb4 Qc5 13.Rxc4 Qxf2+ 14.Kd1 Qxf1+ 15.Kc2 Qxc4+
16.Nc3 f6 17.Be3 Nd6 18.Nf3 Qxg4 0-1

Note that when a game is completed, the result goes in two
places. The result field, and after the last move in the game.
Do not put in the move number either where White resigned
or after Black resigns. The result is not considered a move
and, therefore, should not be recorded as such. This is not
correct PGN notation. Also, this should be written in the same
format as it is in the result field and not in words.

This review of PGN notation was meant to be as informative
as possible. However, I realise there is a lot to correct
notation, particularly on the moves. I therefore encourage you
to ask your New Member Guides if you have any questions on
this. If you have graduated the program (Hooray!) then look in
a chess book. You are allowed to refer to chess books for
reference for something like this. You may not use a computer
program, though! You may also ask your TD if you have a
question. That is what they are there for—to help clear up
matters like this.

I hope you found this review of PGN notation informative
and helpful. I would also like to thank the IECC members who
gave their permission for me to use their names and games.

IECC *(www.geocities.com/Colosseum/Midfield/1254)*

C/ Websites

1) Caissa's Web ****
caissa.com
Headers: *Member Workspace, Live Game Room, Tournament
Hall, Member Directories, Caissa's Library, Caissa's Cafe,
Caissa's Chess Shop*

Pricecheck: *Premium Membership US$50.00/year,
Standard Membership US$25.00/year,* Genius in Chess
US$19.00/ $18.05 (members)

Caissa's Web offers a generous 30-day free trial
membership, and its annual fees are very reasonable, with
special deals for GMs and IMs. Premium membership

includes membership of GM Gabriel Schwartzman's Internet Chess Academy with access to monthly live lectures, as well as the chance to participate in monthly prize tournaments. Plenty of people have taken the plunge—the site claims to host over 2,500 live games per day—so you won't have to wait long to find an opponent.

The Java interface is attractively designed and easy to use, but one unusual aspect of it is that you have to click on a chess clock every time you make a move. In a way this makes the game more realistic because if you forget to press your clock, you lose time, but it's trickier to press a clock using a mouse than it is in real life, and it can cause strain on the wrist. All in all, the manual clock is a gimmick that Caissa's Web would do well to drop. The bulletin board allows members to post bizarre messages such as the following from The Raven: "I'm looking for correspondence games where one is willing to discuss, learn, or teach about deep theological issues such as religion, Christ, the Bible, evolution, world views, etc."

2) Chessed **
www.chessed.com

Headers: *Play, Games, Help, Info, List, E-Mail*

The lucky few who are able to access the Chessed playing arena are probably having a riotous time, but most visitors will be deterred by the incredibly slow loading procedure. The difficulty with live games does not apply to e-mail games—you just have to register and request an opponent—but you don't have any choice over who you play.

3) ChessLive! *
www.chesslive.com

Headers: *Small, Standings, Help, Awards*

Very few people play on this simple site which only offers one-to-one encounters, no tournaments, and they are probably all friends of webmaster Francesco Bosia. But it's all free, and it works.

4) chess.net ****
www.chess.net

Headers: *Play Chess, Chess Shop, News, Events and Tournaments, Photo Gallery*

Pricecheck: *Annual Gold Membership US$49.95, chess.net for Windows CD $49.95, The Roman Forum (Blue) video Volume 1: Dzindzi Indian Defense $29.95*

It is now possible to play on chess.net for free in two different ways—either by downloading the customised software or by using the Java interface. The interface for download is beautifully designed with an adjustable board and a booming American voice which announces "Check!", "Checkmate!" and "White lost on time!" You can chat live, visit various 'rooms', such as the TeenChat Room and the Russian Room, enter tournaments and follow big international events. But not much help is given—for instance, it is not clear how two people sharing the same computer can be allocated different handles, as the administrators are paranoid about duplicates.

If you pay for Gold Membership or for the chess.net software, you get more advanced features and the chance to earn Gold Points which can be exchanged for freebies. There are always plenty of people on chess.net and the website can be accessed in six different European languages. Every Sunday there is a simul by GM Roman Dzindzichashvili or another titled player against 20 opponents.

5) ChessWeb *
studwww.rug.ac.be/~mjdbruyn/chessweb
Headers: *None (icons only)*

Incredibly, over 1,600 games have been played on this site despite the fact that only one game takes place at a time and you have to wait five minutes between moves. A student at the University of Gent in Belgium set up ChessWeb to show what he could do. It's a clever program, but you don't get much of a game. All you can do is make a move in a multi-player game, and there is nothing to stop players from making a move for White and then switching to Black later on, which makes the whole thing rather silly. As it's slow going, people tend to leave cute messages with their moves such as "busy again today, but a move here n there... sunny n hot in Carolina".

6) ECTool *****
www.ectool.nu
Headers: *Introduction, Features, About the author, Download software, Beta versions, Buddychess, Rebel engines, Register on line, FAQ, ECTool tournaments, Notice Board, References, Players list*

Pricecheck: *ECTool 15.00 euros, Rebel 10 Engine for ECTool 10.00 euros, ECTool + Rebel 10 Engine for ECTool 25.00 euros*

Andres Valverde, an agricultural engineer from Spain, has produced the Rolls Royce of e-mail chess software—and it can be purchased for a derisory sum. If you're sceptical, a limited version can be downloaded for a trial period. ECTool allows you to keep a database of games in a similar format to ChessBase, with the facility to add annotations and to keep track of the time elapsed between moves. A Wizard helps you organise tournament games that are taking place simultaneously and there is an e-mail client with address book which can import or export games in PGN format. The software is multilingual, offering the choice of English, Spanish, French, German, Italian, Catalan, and Portuguese.

All the main e-mail chess organisations recommend that their members use ECTool. Valverde also runs his own tournaments and provides a long list of potential opponents with their ELO ratings and e-mail addresses, headed by CC GM Jean Hebert from Canada. Recently Valverde upgraded ECTool and made another program available for free on his site, Buddychess, a sleek interface for playing live. There is only one unsolved mystery here—what possible use could the Rebel 10 analysis engine be to an e-mail player? Well, perhaps you'll want to analyse your games when they're finished...

7) Free Internet Chess Server ****
www.freechess.org

Headers: *Quick Guide, Login Now, Download, Register, Server Info, Sponsors, Help, Mamer*

In its early days, the Internet Chess Club was free of charge. When its administrators decided to introduce a membership fee, some players were outraged and stormed off to create the Free Internet Chess Server. Thus FICS is quite similar to ICC, except that there are fewer players on FICS, fewer events, fewer game options, and everything looks rather amateurish.

FICS doesn't have its own customised graphical interface —you can use JavaBoard, which does the job with no frills attached, and the pieces move annoyingly slowly—or you can download an interface from a long list which doesn't shed much light on the merits of each one. The positive aspect of the site is that everything is free, as advertised, you get a rating and you can play in tournaments with various rules and time controls. FICS offers various wild variants, including bughouse and suicide chess; as well as group analysis, simuls and live coverage of big events such as Sarajevo 2000, which featured Kasparov, Shirov, Morozevich and Adams.

8) ICC *****
www.chessclub.com

Headers: *Newcomers, Members, Help, Register for a Free 7 Day Trial, Clubhouse, Java Interfaces, Chess Store, Events, User Guide, BlitzIn Manual*

Pricecheck: *Annual membership US$49.00/$24.50 (students), ICC Beefy T-Shirt $16.00 plus $3.00 shipping outside USA, Canada and Mexico*

Whether your name is Neuron, Godspell, coffeeisgood, Porno, murky, SlugBucket, Slim-Jim, BostonStrangler,

Severed, CyberTal, Botvinnik, SloppyDefender, BeachCafeChamp, MrChessBoy, ParalyseCabbage, SnailPeel, Apocalyptic, ChariotsofFire, MrCheese or JellyRoll, you will find a suitable opponent on the Internet Chess Club. You meet the weirdest people here (73,076 games are played per day), but don't worry, because you can't see them and they can't see you. You hide behind a 'handle', a mask of anonymity—unless you want to reveal your identity, in which case you can use your real name, or you can leave a message in your 'notes' so that people can read about you and your interests. Type 'finger TheLoser', for example, and you will find that he/she has a FIDE rating of 2257, is from Istanbul, and that "Kocho is the best player I have known personally:)". You might be playing a blitz game with 20 seconds left on your clock, when your opponent whistles at you and says, "Hi, I'm from Alabama, 12 years old, how old are you?" By the time you've composed a reply ("Hi, I'm 43, currently orbiting the Earth in the Mir space station"), your flag has fallen. But the feeling that you are part of a huge, noisy, uninhibited, invisible community with nothing in common except chess, is what makes ICC so much fun.

To start playing on ICC, you go to the homepage and download the BlitzIn software, which provides you with an on-screen chessboard for playing, watching and analysing games (it can have 2D or 3D pieces, a wooden or marble board, and you can choose the sound effects for moves and challenges), and a background window in which players make their challenges and ICC makes its announcements. You can log on as a guest and play for seven days without paying, but none of your games will be rated. The membership fee is extremely reasonable, considering that it gives you a year's unlimited playing time (individual games, tournaments and simuls against GMs), plus access to lectures, interviews and coverage of major events such as Linares 1999. For some special events, members have to pay a little extra; ICC has its own currency, the chekel (worth one US dollar), and you can buy chekels using your credit card. But most live coverage is absolutely free.

One of the big events organised by ICC itself was the Oz.com Qualifier blitz tournament in March 2000, when GM Alex Wojtkiewicz won $500 and entry to the 'Top of the World' tournament in Iceland, which featured Kasparov, Anand, Timman, Korchnoi, Sokolov and six Icelandic GMs. A total of 63 GMs, including Short, Adams, Svidler and Gulko played in the qualifier. The ICC set records for the number of people logged in (2,615), the number of FIDE-titled players logged in (168) and the number of simultaneous games being played (810). The ICC Library contains games from most of the top-level events since 1996, and great historical events such as world championships.

The support service that ICC provides to members is superb—when you join, you receive an e-mail which explains the main ICC commands. If you need extra help after that, then you can type 'info' for a list of subjects, or talk to an administrator online, or ring the administrator who is responsible for your country. Further e-mails are sent out regularly with the results of tournaments and details of forthcoming events. New versions of the BlitzIn software are produced from time to time, and these can be downloaded from ICC so that everyone has the latest technology.

If you live in the United States, you have an advantage, of course, because you don't run up a phone bill while you're on the Internet. Otherwise you may prefer blitz or lightning ('bullet') games to standard time controls, so that you're online for an hour instead of five hours. But you can specify exactly what time limit you want. If you type 'seek 3 2', that means you want to play three minutes each plus two seconds per move. During a blitz game you will find the most annoying problem is 'lag', when there is a delay while your move is being transmitted to your opponent, or vice versa. In this situation both clocks stop, and you have no idea when they are going to start again—so even if you each only have five seconds left, you could be staring at the screen for a minute or more, waiting for your opponent's move to show so that you can react instantaneously. And lag can make it seem as if your opponent has lost on time, because he has a minus number of seconds left, but his automatic flag won't fall and his actual time will be added on when he makes a move. It's frustrating. If the lag is particularly bad, the best thing to do is to leave ICC for a while and come back later. Fortunately, the move timestamping facility ensures that the clocks take lag into account. Before timestamping, you could call your opponent's flag during a delay and be branded a 'lag-flagger', a heinous sin.

When you're fed up with traditional chess, there is an excellent range of 'wild' chess variants available on ICC, as well as bughouse (exchange chess), for four people. You might have to wait a long time for a bughouse partner and for two opponents, so it is worth checking out wild23—Crazyhouse—which is a similar game for two players. When you take an opponent's piece it appears on your screen and when it's your turn to move, you can pick the spare piece up with your mouse and place it on a vacant square. A pawn can be more powerful than a piece in this situation—if you put in on the seventh rank! Fischer-Random chess was also introduced recently (wild22), the game promoted by Bobby Fischer, in which the pieces are arranged randomly on the back rank. Other wild variants include Kriegspiel (wild16), where you can't see your opponent's moves, and Losers' Chess (wild17), where you try to lose all your pieces.

Regular blitz tournaments are organised by computers, notably Tomato and WildOne, who call for a certain number of players and arrange the pairings. This happens fairly quickly, although you might have to wait a while between rounds, especially if one or more of the matches are suffering from severe lag. The tournaments provide an opportunity for weaker players to get games with stronger players, because people who are hundreds of rating points above you are unlikely to agree to an individual game (they will even abort the game sometimes if they accidentally end up playing you), but in a tournament they have no choice. The same goes for the 'King of the Hill' feature. A computer announces that so-and-so is King of the Hill, and anyone can challenge him, winning the title if they win the game. There's nothing in this except kudos, but that counts for a lot on ICC—it's easy to get your 15 minutes of fame one way or another. If you really can't do it by winning games, you can always 'shout' something to everyone who is logged on, perhaps provoking a heated debate on Judit Polgar's marriage prospects or the merits of the Corn Stalk Defence. People who become abusive will be punished by ICC administrators, however.

Even if a GM won't play a game with you, there is nothing to stop you chatting with famous players. There is a directory of titled players on ICC which includes the following GMs:

A-Baburin/IrishBear—Alexander Baburin, Ireland
A-Khalifman—Alexander Khalifman, Russia
A-Morozevich—Alexander Morozevich, Russia
airgun—Aaron Summerscale, England
AttackGM—Julian Hodgson, England
BERTA—Ulf Andersson, Sweden
Bradidik—Eugene Torre, Philippines
chaozz—Sergei Movsesian, Czech Republic
DaveNoGood—David Norwood, England
DeanAshley—Maurice Ashley, USA
DGurevich—Dmitry Gurevich, USA
Dlugy—Maxim Dlugy, USA
E-Sutovsky/GMAlex—Emil Sutovsky, Israel
EasyToGuess—Joel Lautier, France
Flash-Gordon—Dorian Rogozenko, Moldova
FlyingPiket—Jeroen Piket, Netherlands
gahan—Babakuli Annakov, Turkmenistan
gasch—Gabriel Schwartzman, USA
Gatotkaca—Utut Adianto, Indonesia
Henley—Ron Henley, USA
juliana/ReindermanD—Dmitri Reinderman, Netherlands
junior—Ilya Gurevich, USA
KingLoek—Loek van Wely, Netherlands
Leon—Alexei Shirov, Spain
Lombardy—William Lombardy, USA
Mgur—Mikhail Gurevich, Belgium

Mihail—Mikhail Saltaev, Uzbekistan
MikeOfLandsberg—Michal Krasenkow, Poland
Mishtatef—Jonathan Mestel, England
MrHat—Joel Benjamin, USA
NDShort—Nigel Short, England
Parsifal/Beatrice—James Plaskett, England
PBS/p-svidler—Peter Svidler, Russia
Psakhis—Lev Psakhis, Israel
Ree—Hans Ree, Netherlands
Rubi—Valery Salov, Russia
Securitron—Jonathan Tisdall, Norway
Shirav—Dashzevegin Sharavdorj, Mongolia
Speelman—Jonathan Speelman, England
Tioro—Tal Shaked, USA
TonyM—Tony Miles, England
Vagr—Vladimir Akopian, Armenia
WBrowne—Walter Browne, USA
Yermo—Alex Yermolinsky, USA
Z-Almasi—Zoltan Almasi, Hungary

By typing 'finger' and a player's handle you can sometimes find out interesting facts about them, or you may be treated to their original brand of humour, or presented with an advertisement for chess services. Here are some highlights:

A-Morozevich
1 My ELO is my only glory. Respect it please—no foolish challengers, especially from the strong opponents
2 I am renting out my handle; price is reasonable; mode of payment: any
3 I am completely serious with my 1 and 2 fingernotes. So your proposals are welcome

DaveNoGood
1 Dave Norwood
2 Retired grandmaster... ashamed to keep the title
3 I only play 1 g3 and 1...g6
4 If my play gets a bit funny it may have something to do with what I'm drinking...

E-Sutovsky/GMAlex
1 Emil Sutovsky, Israel
2 I like chatting, especially discussing music and books

NDShort
1 Nigel David Short, born 01/06/65 in Leigh, Lancashire, England
2 Elo 2683
3 Cricket team: The Athenians
4 Right hand bat. Four matches, two innings, one not out, high score 5*, average 10
5 Slow right arm bowler. One over, 10 for no wicket
6 Three catches

Parsifal/Beatrice
1 Hi! James Plaskett, England, ELO 2515, British Champion 1990
2 When appearing on the UK version of *Who Wants To Be A Millionaire?* on Nov 12th 1999, I could not put knuckle, wrist, elbow, shoulder in the correct sequence from fingertips upwards. 20 million people now know I cannot tell my arse from my elbow!
3 Well in fact I DID answer correctly, but my 'C' button was not working! Plus the guy who got on was 0.9 secs faster than me anyway. PLUS I screwed up the 2 other fastest finger rounds. So, unlike NDSHORT and DAVENOGOOD, I am STILL not a 7 figure man!

Securitron
1 stationed in Foreigncountryland
2 Favorite quote: "I don't think like a tree—do you think like a tree?"—Anatoly Lein
3 I have now written a book inspired by Lein and thinking like trees

Tioro
1 Hi! I am Tal Shaked from Tucson, Arizona
2 but sveshi calls me taloro
3 1997 World Junior Champion
4 COYOTE CHESS CAMP (formerly the Wildcat Chess camp) at the University of Arizona (Tucson)

TonyM
1 No, I'm not Tony Miles
2 Well not always...
3 I prefer to play blitz with a beautiful woman and a bottle of wine in front of a log fire...
4 please bring your own logs

For communication with GMs, IMs and the rank-and-file on ICC, there are 300 channels which can be switched on or off according to your tastes. There are channels for discussion of chess theory, general politics, films, music, maths and science, sport, and various language channels including Spanish, Russian, Hebrew and Turkish.

ICC membership is free for GMs and IMs who make their names public. When a GM logs on to ICC, his presence is announced to everyone by the administrators, and there are frequent messages letting you know which GMs and IMs are playing each other, so that you can follow their games—and kibitz. One of the most frequent visitors is Pablo Zarnicki (garompon), who often gives simuls and will teach you via the Internet in English or Spanish for 40 chekels an hour. If you type 'help services' you can see a list of all the players who offer coaching.

Lectures on ICC are a great way to learn, and if you don't want to stay online, members can order transcripts by e-mail. IM Danny Kopec has given several lectures. The computer program MrSpock gives a lecture every hour, on the hour, designed for players of various ability levels. There are 34 different MrSpock lectures, ranging from 'The Winawer Variation of the French Defense' to 'Strategic Petrosian Games' and 'Mr Spock's Crash Course in Rook Endings'. Finally, it is also possible to play correspondence chess on ICC. Games can be saved in your personal library, so that you can keep track of what's happening.

9) ICCF ****
www.iccf.com

Headers: *About ICCF, Statutes, Who is who?, Nations, Titles, Email Chess, Playing rules, Direct Entry, Ratings, Tables, TD reports, Games Archive, Discussions*

Pricecheck: *Email Master Class US$15.00, Email Higher Class $10.00, Email Open Class $10.00*

E-mail has instilled a new lease of life into correspondence chess and the International Correspondence Chess Federation is starting to take advantage of the possibilities. The ICCF has been the official organisation for CC for over 50 years, so it knows what it's doing. Equally, if you join an ICCF event you must be prepared to take it seriously. You are supposed to enter through your country's federation, but if there is no ICCF member federation in your country, you can use the direct entry facility. Contact details for member federations are published on the site. There is also a huge section of results and crosstables. The drawbacks are that there isn't a very wide variety of tournaments to enter yet, and you can't play one-to-one. The design of the site is extremely staid, perhaps intended to ward off the frivolous.

10) IECC *****
www.geocities.com/Colosseum/Midfield/1264

Headers: *Join the IECC, IECC Guidelines, Guidelines (Text), Algebraic Notation, About the IECC, Current Events, Ratings, Absences, Game Reports, Time Violations, Volunteering, Game Archive, Newsletters, Academy, Team Events, Knockout Matches, Pyramid Ladder, Class Events, Swiss Open, 2-Game/Trios, 1-Game Matches, Thematics, Chess Software, Staff Photo Album*

The International E-mail Chess Club offers a superb choice of events and provides a one-to-one tutorial service for newcomers. And it's all completely free. The IECC newsletters create a link between members and a forum for analysing games, reviewing books and publicising your local chess scene—in one issue, Jesus Paul from Spain writes about Club de Ajedrez Valladolid, where he plays, Steve Ryan from Canada lists his favourite chess trivia and quotes, and Gertjan de Vries from the Netherlands reviews *Winning with the Smith-Morra Gambit*. IECC is becoming more and more popular, but it has cut down its waiting lists for a practice game and has introduced a Fast Tracker System for experienced e-mail players.

11) IECG *****
www.iecg.org
Headers: *Newsletters, Rules, IECG Staff, Vacation list, Forum, Registration, Tutorial Office, Join Tournaments, Class Tournaments waiting lists, Thematic, Events, Rating List, Tournament Results, Game archives, Change of Address*

The International E-mail Chess Group is a little more formal than IECC, but otherwise there is little to choose between the two organisations. IECG runs hundreds of tournaments every year, including the IECG Cup and IECG World Championship, in which participants compete for prizes donated by ChessBase. The IECG site is enlivened by book reviews and the Web Watcher section, where other chess sites are scrutinised.

12) Internet Chess Players **
www.webgenerations.com/icp
Headers: *Register with ICP, News, Member Directory, Chess Ladder, cgiCHESS (Live), Tournament Info, Email Chess, Chat Room, Message Board, Guestbook Services, Underground Chess Network (UCN), Frequently Asked Questions*

This muddled, badly-designed site does actually offer the opportunity to play live and by e-mail, but not many people bother. To play live you sit down at a table and make a move on a game that is already in progress. If a game hasn't started, presumably you could contact a friend who happens to be online and get them to sit down at the table with you, but it might be easier simply to ask someone living nearby to give you a game in person! There is a list of contacts for people to arrange casual e-mail games between themselves, from webwacker (Adam Lawson), who is the founder of ICP from Los Angeles and likes "quotes, boats, computer stuff, backgammon, checkers and chess", to Sauron, "a 14-year-old cyborg who's addicted to computers. I've tried several help groups but my addiction is much too strong. I also play lots of sports (mainly hockey, soccer, skiing, golf and tennis) and am very smart." ICP does occasionally run tournaments with "AWSOME" (sic) prizes.

13) ItsYourTurn.com **
www.itsyourturn.com

>Headers: *Help, Play, Talk, Spy, Account, Visitors, Info*

>ItsYourTurn.com boasts over 210,000 registered users who are playing backgammon, checkers, Battleship, Stack4, reversi, Go-Moku and other games as well as chess. Once you've created a free user-id, you can enter the Waiting Room and see if there are any chess players looking for a game. Some give their official rating; some just say they are a beginner, intermediate or advanced player; others give no indication of their strength. Usually there are one or two chess players in the Waiting Room, and you can start a game by making a move on someone's board, or by making a move on your own board and waiting for a random person to reply. You don't stay online while you're waiting, but are notified by e-mail when it's your turn to move. There is no time limit, and there are no organised events, just individual games. You can leave messages for your opponents, but you can't e-mail them directly unless you can persuade them to give you their e-mail address. It's a simple way to play a friendly correspondence game, without the hassles of officialdom or the reward of an improved rating.

14) MindSports **
www.mindsports.net

>Headers: *The Arena, The Strategy Shop, I Ching Connexion*

>Pricecheck: *Grand Chess Board US$39.00 plus $30.00 shipping & handling, Grand Chess Pieces $49.00 plus same shipping & handling*

>You can play or watch e-mail chess here on a Java board, but nothing much is organised—you just pick an opponent from the list and start a game. Grand Chess, on a 10x10 board, is also available, along with other 'mind sports' such as Emergo, SuperStar and Othello. Probably the best feature on the site for chess players is the opportunity in the Shop to download Alexei Bartashnikov's Chess Learning Programs, which are designed to improve your skills of piece movement, capturing sequences, mating nets and visualization.

15) MSN Gaming Zone ***
www.zone.com/chess

>Headers: *Getting Started, News, Ratings, Tournaments & Events, Game Shop, Downloads, Chat, Social Rooms, Competitive Rooms, Ladder Rooms, Rated Rooms, Tournament Rooms*

>The Kasparov vs. The World event in 1999 was played on Microsoft's games site, and thousands logged on to suggest a

move or just to watch the gripping contest. As a result of the publicity, you will find between 500 and 600 players at any one time in the 15 chess rooms. One of the deterrents, however, is the Gaming Zone's bulky software which takes a long time to download. What you get for your efforts is animated tables where your cartoon alter ego can sit down with an opponent or on its own to await a game, and a 'Friends' box which indicates when someone you know is online. The 3D pieces are nifty, but there's no 'takeback' or time increment option and you can't examine the game afterwards. Chess on this site is likely to be appreciated most by hardened computer games players who rate cool graphics above the subtleties of the game.

16) MSO Worldwide **
www.msoworld.com

Headers: *What's New, Mindzine, Play Games Online, Message Boards, IQ Tests, Puzzles, Creative Thinking, Mind Sports Olympiad, About MSO, MSO Jobs, Press Releases, Praise for our site, Chat*

The Mind Sports Olympiad has been held annually in London since 1997, and this is the website that complements the event (slogan: "Bringing brains together"). The joint webmasters are computer programmer David Levy and GM Jonathan Tisdall, who edits the 'Mindzine'. The site is quite useful in terms of news, with different sections for the diverse range of games hosted here, and it covers everything from financial crisis in the US Chess Federation to the results of the latest supertournament, with games to download. But the playing software is very poor, which might explain why sometimes all the games rooms are empty.

If you are the only person in a room you can challenge a 'robot', choosing the level of difficulty, but every time you pick up a piece, annoying spots appear on all the possible squares you can move to, and you can't change your mind about which piece you're going to move, even in a blitz game. Theoretically the software can cope with a number of chess variants, if anyone turns up to play them. The most original feature on this site is the Chess Horoscope, which predicts for Aries, "The first half of July will be rainy, on the chessboard and off", and for Gemini, "Blitz chess is your game now! No one can keep up with you, lots of poor sports left in the dust." Most amusing, albeit not exactly aimed at the higher end of the IQ scale.

17) Nikos Chesspage **
home.snafu.de/niko/games/chess.html

Headers: *Help, Create New Game, Watch Games in Progress, Watch Ladder Games in Progress, Watch*

Championship Games in Progress, Find a Partner in the Discussion Board

Thanks to Niko, you can play a friendly game here or take part in a tournament without downloading a graphical interface. The pieces are oddly shaped, but that's the only real quibble with the board's appearance, and the clock with moving hands is a clever gimmick. You start with a credit of 20 days for all your moves and gain an extra day for every move you make. There isn't a very long list of potential opponents on the Discussion Board, though, and some messages have been festering there for 18 months or so. It needs some editing, Niko.

18) PacMall Online Chess ***
www.pacific-mall.com/games/chess

Headers: *My Account, Team Chess, Honors 1 On 1, Snoop, 1 On 1, Misc.*

The PacMall site is improving, but it won't make the hordes come charging in quite yet. You estimate how many moves you will make per week, find an opponent and play e-mail chess on a board which isn't Java and doesn't have to be downloaded. That's it. Or you can join in a free-for-all game where anyone can make a move, with a general board in the Lobby as well as ratings-limited boards for stronger players only.

19) UECC *****
www.lobocom.es/~ebailen/cmain.html

Headers: *Francisco Bailén, Index, UECC, Join, Rules, ELO System, UECC Members, Players, Rating, Friendly, Thematics, Pyramid, Events, Analysis, Download Zone, Chess-Tool 2000, Leisure, Services, Suggestions, Chess Books, FORUM*

Pricecheck: *UECC Membership 1,000 Spanish pesetas/ US$8.00/7.00 euros*

The young founder of the Universal E-mail Chess Club, Francisco Bailén, died from cystic fibrosis in October 1999 and the site now contains a tribute to him as well as some of his games. Activities are still continuing and it's all free, but the small membership fee brings additional benefits such as a 10 per cent discount on Spanish chess books, the right to play in tournaments with prizes, and games collections sent to you by e-mail. All information on the site is in English and Spanish, and there is no induction procedure—you simply sign up and start playing, either in an organised event or by challenging someone to an individual game. The following types of events are available: Closed, Quads, Knockout,

Teams, Nations (in which players from a particular country compete to be national champion), Pyramid, Thematics, Friendly and UECC Tournaments.

20) WCCF *****
www.geocities.com/radale/wccf/menu.htm

Headers: *JOIN Our Friendly Chess Family, New Member REGISTRATION, RULES & Procedures, Rating FORMULA, Frequently Asked QUESTIONS, Email Chess EVENTS, ECTOOL Game Recorder, New Event REQUEST, Member RATINGS, Match RESULTS, Event STATUS, Federation NEWSLETTER, Time COMPLAINT Report, COMPLETED Game Report, Member FEEDBACK, Sample MESSAGE Format, Sample ASSIGNMENT Format, Amusing Chess QUOTES*

The excellent e-mail chess site NOST (kNights Of the Square Table) transformed itself into the World Correspondence Chess Federation, and then, in April 2000, its founder Ronleigh Dale died. Like UECC, the site is continuing to function, with its efficiently organised events and friendly participants. When you register, you are assigned a 'tutor', who will play two simultaneous practice games with you until he is satisfied that you understand PGN-format and are following the rules. Then the games are abandoned and you can immediately enter one of the tournaments: King (15 players), Marshall (9 players), Queen (7 players), Cardinal (6 players, 2 games each), Rook (5 players), Bishop (4 players, 2 games each), Knight (3 players, 2 games each), Pawn (2 players, 2 games each) or Pyramid (2 players).

Your tutor may criticise you severely, for omitting a move number or forgetting to type your e-mail address at the bottom of the message, but in a real event you'll probably find that players don't worry too much about the odd slip-up. If you're careful, you won't have to play many moves with your tutor before you're deemed ready to join an event. WCCF member Stanley Bass has added some light entertainment to the site with his 'Amusing Chess QUOTES', which includes the wisdom of Reuben Fine, "I'd rather have a pawn than a finger", and Siegbert Tarrasch, "When you don't know how to play—wait for an idea to come into your opponent's mind. You may be sure that idea will be false."

21) World Chess Network ****
www.117.gotochess.com/English/welcome.php3
Headers: *Welcome, Play Chess, Lecture Series, Banter Chess, Chess History*

This brand new site is owned and operated by Master Games International Inc., a corporation founded in 1997 by a group of high achievers: "The Chairman is Bill Church, a founder and long time Chairman of North America's successful Church's Chicken. The President is Robert Hamilton, who staged the 1988 World Chess Festival, North America's largest and most prestigious chess event. The Senior Technology Planner is Marty Hirsch, winner of a NASA award for work on the Voyager Space Mission and several World Championships for developing the world's strongest chess playing software. The Honorary Chairman is Dato Tan Chin Nam, a wealthy Asian businessman who served as Deputy President of the International Chess Federation. Legendary World Chess Champion, Boris Spassky, who twice battled eccentric American genius, Bobby Fischer, is International Ambassador."

So, does the site live up to the reputation of its creators? Well, it hasn't started badly. The software is quick to download and easy to use. The way the registration procedure works, players are often enticed into giving their real names, which means you can guess what nationality they are and you're more likely to get involved in a conversation here than you would on ICC with someone calling themselves DarthVader or SneakyPawn. There are usually under 100 people logged on at any particular time, but numbers will probably increase as the site becomes better known.

It's free to play and to watch the lectures or 'Banter Chess' games between GMs and IMs such as Larry Christiansen, John Fedorowicz, Doru Rogozenko and Tomas Hutters. Lectures are self-explanatory, while banter chess is where the two strong players comment live during their games. Once you've registered, you automatically receive the schedules for lectures and banter chess by e-mail, and you can select which time zone you're living in, so that you don't have to work out the actual playing times yourself.

The only below-par section of the site is the single page on chess history. The first millennium-and-a-half of chess is dismissed in what must be a record nine lines, which include the dubious piece of trivia that in Europe, "in order to be Knighted, it helped if you played a good game of chess". Slaying dragons and rescuing damsels in distress presumably weren't rated as highly as we thought they were in the sedate, intellectual Middle Ages! Then we gallop straight through to a paragraph on the Fischer-Spassky match, which "attracted more journalists than the 1988 Winter Olympics"; and the remaining four paragraphs are devoted to Kasparov vs. Deep Blue and Kasparov vs. the World. NASA won't be giving the World Chess Network any prizes for history, but who knows, maybe this version of events could be turned into a Hollywood blockbuster, with Sean Connery as a chess-playing Sir Lancelot and Mel Gibson as Kasparov...

22) Yahoo! Games ****
games.yahoo.com

Headers: *Board Games, Card Games, Tile Games, Other Games*

Chess is hosted for free by the immensely popular search engine Yahoo!, along with a wide range of other games including backgammon, reversi, mahjong, canasta and poker. You have to sign up with Yahoo! first, which doesn't take long and automatically gives you an e-mail address as well. The Java chess interface on Yahoo! is straightforward to use, with on-screen instructions, the main problem being that the pieces move rather slowly and your clock runs down in the meantime. Sit down at a table with a player who is waiting for a game or choose an empty table and set your own parameters such as rating and time limits. If you don't like your opponent you can 'boot' them off your table unceremoniously. When a game is finished, there is an option to have the score sent to you by e-mail.

Yahoo! sometimes has over 4,000 people playing chess at once in games rooms, which are divided into beginner, intermediate, advanced and ladder rooms; with names like Camel Club, Owl Tree, Amoeba Drop and Pelican Palace. For the more loquacious types you can not only chat live, but also contribute to one of the numerous message boards on topics from "All cheaters can go to hell!" to "Play chess over e-mail, beginner please". It's not sophisticated, but there's something for everyone.

D/ Newsgroups

rec.games.chess.play-by-email ****

This is the right place to come if you are daunted by the strict rules of correspondence or e-mail chess organisations and just want to arrange a friendly game independently. Lots of people leave messages asking for opponents, often giving their first move, or specifying a particular opening they want to play. The helpful Frequently Asked Questions posting from the person who maintains the newsgroup, 'Paul Morphy', explains things like PGN, algebraic notation and the use of computers in e-mail chess tournaments. Notices from e-mail chess organisations are also posted here, in case you want to go further.

5
Chess History

There is a wealth of chess history on the Internet and many historical sites are reviewed in the next chapter, **Archives and Databases**, because their primary purpose is to preserve the games of the past. The sites in this chapter mainly contain historical articles, with the ever-growing Chess Café, being the best by a mile. Bill Wall, on the other hand, values humour more than accuracy.

A/ Webmaster Hall of Fame

Hanon Russell, The Chess Café

Please introduce yourself

My wife and I live in Milford, Connecticut, a coastal town of about 50,000 located about 65 miles east of New York City. I am 52 years old and an attorney specializing in commercial real estate and business law.

How serious a chess player are you?

I have been playing tournament chess since I was about 11 or 12 years old. I suppose you would call me fairly serious,

Hungary Gallery Listing

although, like many others, I do not get a chance to play as often as I would like. I hold a US national master's rating in the 2220-2230 range.

When and why did you decide to set up a website?

From 1989 until about 1992 or 1993, I had reviewed books and done a few related things on the old Linc Network, a.k.a. the USA Today Sports Center. In late December 1995, I read an article about setting up a website and pursued it. Around that time I had also made the decision to explore the possibility of selling some of the documents in my collection. It all seemed to fit together. I have also known that there has long been a need for honest book reviewing on a regular basis and wanted to see what could be done on the World Wide Web in this regard.

Did you have any technical problems?

At first I had no idea what was going on. I hired a firm based in San Diego (some 3,000 miles away) and they did everything. The distance was not a great problem, since everything was transmitted electronically. It not only became very expensive to do everything that way, but there was an absence of control that left me feeling somewhat helpless and the site somewhat sluggish in responding to errors, readers, etc. I was struggling to find the right combination to present to readers/visitors. We officially opened online on April 1, 1996; the first month had a grand total of 15,000 hits (not visits). I figured most were due to me and my family and a few others who had stumbled upon the site by mistake.

The technical aspects were at first quite intimidating, but we soon established a routine and the site began to come into its own, albeit in fits and starts. Most sites then and now are basically reflections of work done in hard copy—i.e., a traditional print magazine will establish a site to promote its subscriptions, giving visitors a glimpse into what they can expect and related information. My idea was to present original material, available nowhere else. But I soon realised that book reviews were not enough. After two months online, I contacted Tim Harding and arranged for him to write an original column each month. This was a stroke of very good luck. Tim is a terrific chess journalist and although I had had no prior direct contact with him, he agreed.

That was followed shortly by Dutch GM Hans Ree joining The Chess Café as a regular columnist. Hans and I knew each other and in fact he had stayed at our home during his previous visit to the US, and we stayed with him and his wife when we visited Amsterdam. Tim and Hans became the early core columnists online. In my opinion, they are both outstanding chess journalists. They were the only two journalists for about a year. The site, at that time, presented historical items from my collection, an occasional miscellaneous item, and, perhaps the linchpin of the site, weekly book reviews. I have thought for years that there is a need for honest book reviews. There are a relatively large number of chess books published each year and most are described by either publishers or dealers who want to sell the same books. But the independent review is rare.

The reviews I had been doing on the Linc were very well received. Of course, there were the predictable knee-jerk reactions: I was a genius in the eyes of the publisher when praising its books, an idiot when panning them. But the readers responded very well and I carried the book reviews forward when establishing the site. By the end of 1996, the site was slowly but surely establishing itself as a place where some interesting original journalism could be found, along with a few unique items, including the presentation, one game per week, of Botvinnik's four-volume autobiographical game collection.

However, soon after that, Botvinnik's heirs demanded that the presentation stop, alleging violation of copyright. This in spite of the fact that I had written permission from the Soviet copyright agency (VAAP) to translate and publish it. I was tempted to do battle in court with them, but I was more interested in focusing on the site. I dropped the games when negotiations (again!) for the rights broke down and substituted an endgame study section, which has become extremely popular.

It was just about this time that I made the commitment to see how far I could carry the idea of publishing new material online. In other words, the site was not going to be auxiliary to a hard copy book or magazine endeavour, nor was it going to be an egocentric whim. It was going to be a serious journalistic effort, publishing original material online.

Without knowing much at all about the technical end of things, I assumed full control of the technical production of the site at the end of 1996. I am not embarrassed to admit that within the next few months, I made almost every conceivable technical error associated with publishing online. It was quite a learning experience. However, I mastered some sophisticated software (e.g. FrontPage, Photoshop), taught myself HTML scripting, at least at a basic useable level, and even acquired some ability to produce enhancing graphics.

During the first half of 1997, I refined, tweaked and stabilized the presentation. Then, in the second half of 1997, I was quite fortunate to double the number of regular columnists by having Edward Winter and Burt Hochberg come on board. Hochberg was a former editor of *Chess Life,* while Winter was already an established and respected chess writer. In addition, Glenn Budzinski joined me in the book review section.

By the end of the second half of 1997, it was clear to me that things were beginning to come together quite nicely. The addition of Winter and Hochberg complemented Harding and Ree and with Budzinski now assuming responsibility for some of the reviews, my time could be devoted to maintaining and improving the quality of the site. Things then began to fast-track...

In the first six months of 1998, the number of columnists doubled again. Susan Lalic, Geurt Gijssen, Richard Forster and Sunil Weeramantry joined us in rapid succession. Much to my delight, they were all very well received. Within another year, we had a dozen columnists, including British opening specialist, IM Gary Lane; Dutch master and author, Tim Krabbé; former editor of *Inside Chess* Mike Franett; 3-time US champion GM Lev Alburt; the former executive director of the US Chess Federation, Al Lawrence; Danish FM Carsten Hansen; renowned chess author, Bruce Pandolfini; British GM Tony Miles; and Australian master Chris Depasquale. It is a very popular, albeit eclectic, group of writers.

How do you choose your columnists/what material to have on the site; is there anything you wouldn't publish?

Sometimes I choose my writers; sometimes they choose me. The first four to join The Chess Café—Harding, Ree, Winter and Hochberg—were all well-known, respected chess journalists. When the timing was appropriate, I asked them if they would be interested in writing a monthly column and they agreed. These were not difficult decisions for me to make. I felt fortunate to be able to afford to present quality columns by experienced writers.

Things then became more complicated. Having established a base of what I considered very good writers, I wanted to look for one or more relatively unique columns that would retain interest for our readers. It came to my attention that although magazines worldwide were awash with regular columns and articles by male GMs, there did not seem to be a regular column written by a woman. That became my next priority.

I had discussions with several women about the possibility of writing such a column. It is my opinion that any old IM or GM can knock off an average column of 1,200 words, annotating a game or two, throwing in a few interesting notes, and yadda-yadda-yadda. All very common. An annotated game or two was acceptable, but I wanted a woman's point of view of chess playing at the higher international levels. Finally Jonathan Manley (editor and publisher of the fine satirical chess magazine *Kingpin*) recommended the British Women's Champion Susan Lalic, and she joined The Chess Café shortly thereafter.

She was followed by Geurt Gijssen as a regular columnist. During the 1980s, I had become good friends with the American GM Sam Reshevsky. I accompanied Reshevsky to many tournaments, seeing to it that he got kosher food and generally making sure things went smoothly for him. In 1989, when we were at the GMA Qualifying Tournament in Palma de Mallorca, I befriended the Dutch international arbiter, Geurt Gijssen. We became friends and when the first half of the 1990 Kasparov-Karpov World Championship match was held in New York, Gijssen, who was Chief Arbiter for that match, spent most of his weekends at our home.

We remained good friends and at the end of 1997 we explored the possibility of his writing a column for The Chess Café, about the trials and tribulations of being an international arbiter. We met again in Paris in March 1998 and came to an agreement. His very popular column is unlike anything else you will find either online or in standard print.

The 'rules' for my columnists are really quite simple: (1) The column must be about chess (sorry for stating the obvious!); (2) No libel or vulgarity; and (3) No criticism of other Chess Café columnists (I do not need the aggravation of being a referee in a journalistic chess civil war). Other than that, I am a firm believer in free speech and free opinion. I can say that thus far I have never censored any writer at The Chess Café. My editing has always been focused on producing a piece that will interest Chess Café readers.

Are you always looking out for columnists and do you miss any who no longer write for the site?

The curious thing, at least in my opinion, is that I regularly receive enquiries from international masters and grandmasters about the possibility of writing a column for The Chess Café. Perhaps this is standard with other magazines; I don't know. It is an interesting phenomenon. When Susan Lalic's schedule prevented her from continuing as a columnist, I was unable to find another woman to write about women's chess. Edward Winter stopped being a regular columnist in August 1999, but we remain in contact and he has made occasional contributions to The Chess Café.

How useful has the website been for publicizing your business —can you estimate how much money it has made for you?

The public has become used to hearing instant success stories—huge increases in the values of Internet stocks on the stock market. In fact, my experience is that this is much like any other business; or as they say, 95 percent perspiration, five percent inspiration. There is a lot of hard work associated with maintaining a quality site. There are almost two dozen people involved in the writing, production, servicing and maintenance of the site.

We have gradually become recognized as one of the premier content sites for chess on the web. Traffic to the site is approaching 80,000 visits (the equivalent of over a million 'hits') per month and increasing by 3-4 per cent each month. However, the costs are considerable, and while revenue from book and equipment sales is increasing, the site is still technically in the red. Fortunately we are solidly capitalized and are committed to continue bringing original, quality chess content online.

How much feedback do you get from readers, and what are their main criticisms/aspects that they particularly like?

We get a fair amount of feedback from readers. In April 1997, I established a section of The Chess Café called The Bulletin Board, designed specifically to give readers a place to express their opinions, ask questions, etc. Readers submit their comments and, if appropriate, they get posted. I say "if appropriate", because as is explained in the introductory material to The Bulletin Board, I retain the absolute right to edit or refuse to publish anything submitted. Thus the occasionally vulgar or offensive material seen in newsgroups is eliminated. Although on an academic level, this policy of a monitored Bulletin Board could be criticized; given that this is a private site, beholden to no one, and that its goal is to promote and present topics of interest to chess players, I think it is sound.

Why did you decide to bring out a weekly newsletter by e-mail and has this increased interest in the site?

The weekly newsletter was created in May 1997, when I thought that our readers might want to receive a special mailing about what was going on. It has become quite popular, with almost 3,000 recipients each week. It usually contains two or three paragraphs of chit-chat and then a listing of everything that is going on with links that can be activated directly to those pages from the newsletter. There is no question that it has increased interest in the site. We do not use the newsletter for 'spamming' purposes, nor do we make it available to anyone else.

What legal aspects do you have to consider, such as libel or breach of copyright?

The Chess Café honours copyrighted material produced by others without fail. Permission to reprint is always obtained or it is not used. Work submitted by Chess Café journalists is copyrighted in their name, with an overlaying of a blanket copyright—CyberCafes, LLC (the corporation that legally owns and operates the site). We regularly receive requests to reprint material that appears on The Chess Café and we regularly decline such requests.

I take what I think is the common sense approach to this: I pay each writer every month for his or her work and I expect it to appear exclusively at The Chess Café. (The one notable exception to this policy is Hans Ree's column, which has usually appeared a few weeks earlier in Dutch in his column in NRC-Handelsblad.) Therefore, although it is flattering to have someone request it, I politely but firmly refuse to allow reprints. I have agreed that the writer may use the material, but only four to six months, at least, after it was published online. It should be pointed out that every writer is aware of this policy before his or her articles begin to appear at The Chess Café. If they have a problem with this (and no one has yet), we simply cannot have them writing for The Chess Café. I do not believe that this policy is unfair or unreasonable.

What are your future plans for the site?

The current scope of the site has become rather extensive, while its depth is also substantial. Having said that, I am always open to suggestions, improvements, additions and, if necessary, deletions. The key is flexibility. At the moment, we have technically 12 columnists, five book reviewers (including myself) and numerous freelance contributors. A specialized consulting firm has also been brought on board with the hope and expectation that they can help take us to the next level.

The spontaneity and immediacy of electronic publishing allows me to engage occasionally in some experimentation. So, for example, a while back we featured a thumbnail biographical sketch of Emil Diemer written by Stefan Buecker in the original German, without a translation. In the (English) introduction to the piece, I did explain to the readers that we were looking for their reaction—did they wish to see the odd article in a language other than English or did they want to stay with English only. About 150 people sent in e-mails, with English only, winning by a 60-40 per cent margin. The point is not the reception of a particular article or approach, the point is that these digressions may be taken at all. There is enormous potential and flexibility, and it can and should be explored. I have no problem 'pushing the envelope', as they say.

I would like to expand book and equipment sales and stimulate more interaction with our visitors and readers. Several ideas are under serious consideration; and although I am unable to comment upon them at the present time, perhaps they will have come into fruition by the time these words are read by the public.

Which other sites do you consider to be serious rivals?

My intent from the outset was to have an original online publication, not a spin-off of a traditional print journal. There are good sites out there and sites that present some very interesting material in their own right. Yasser Seirawan has converted his *Inside Chess* magazine to an online journal, and *KasparovChess.com* appeared online earlier this year (2000). I suppose most people would consider these two sites competitors. There is not a lot of original, quality material that is produced on the web. The next few years should see some interesting developments and shake-outs. Stay tuned...

B/ Websites

1) Bill Wall's Chess Page ***
www.geocities.com/SiliconValley/Lab/7378/chess.htm

Headers: *Addicted to Chess (humor), Age of Chess Masters, Alekhine's Defense, Mokele (1 e4 ♘f6 2 e5 ♘e4), Alekhine's Defense, Retreat Variation (1 e4 ♘f6 2 e5 ♘g8), Amar or Paris Opening (1 ♘h3), Annoying Your Opponent—best techniques (humor), Art and Chess (Wall), Automatons of chess—Turk, Ajeeb, Mephisto, Barnes Opening (1 f3), Beavis and Butthead Chess, The Bishop, Blackmar-Diemer Links (1 d4 d5 2 e4 dxe4), Bogart and Chess, Books, New (humor), Bourdonnais-McDonnell match (London, 1834), Budapest Traps, Carr's Defense (1 e4 h6), Chess books written by Bill Wall (26 books), Chess Names (chess pieces in other languages), Chess Olympics, Computer Chess History, Chronology of Chess (Wall), Death of chess players, DEEP BLUE vs Kasparov (match 1), DEEPER BLUE vs Kasparov (match 2—Deeper Blue wins), Definitions in chess (humor), Dunst Opening (1 ♘c3), Durkin's Opening (1 ♘a3), Earliest Chess Games, Eccentric Chess Players, Excuses in chess, Epigrams of Chess (chess quotes and sayings), Famous people who play chess, Firsts in chess, Fischer's tournament and match record, Histogram of chess ratings, Horoscope for chess players (humor), Kasparov Games (recent games), Knight Moves (endings involving a knight), Larsen's Opening (games with 1 b3), Limericks, Losing (Why you lose at chess), Masters of Chess—A Profile, Morphy bio, Morphy's chess links, Morphy's Laws of Chess, Movies With Chess Scenes, Occupations of chess players, Olympics—Chess, Opening Frequency, Opening Names, Orangutan Opening (1 b4) (some short games), Philidor's Defense (1e4 e5 2 ♘f3 d6 (some miniatures), Pickering's defense (1 e4 h5), Postal chess, Principles of Chess, Pronounce that chess word, 2 ♕h5 (1 e4 e5 2 ♕h5), Religion and chess, Resigning in chess (humor), 700 Opening Traps Review, Ruy Lopez, Bird variation, Scotch on the Rocks (1 e4 e5 2 ♘f3 ♘c6 3 d4— some miniatures), Shakespeare and chess, Sicilian, Dragon, Sicilian, Rossolimo Variation (1 e4 c5 2 ♘f3 ♘c6 3 ♗b5), Stamps—Chess, Staunton Chess Design, Staunton vs Saint Amant (Paris 1843), Team Chess Names, Traps and Chess Miniatures (super short chess games), US Chess Champions, Ware's Defense (1 e4 a5), Widow, Chessplayer (humor)*

Pricecheck: *Books by Bill Wall US$7.50*

An eclectic site which is broader than it is deep. The spurious nature of some of the anecdotes, the absence of diagrams, the excessive number of miniatures won on the Internet by Bill Wall, and the recurring advertisements from GeoCities, are all drawbacks which ought to be remedied. Nevertheless, there is some fun reading here. Wall concludes that Shakespeare must have been a chess fanatic because of the number of chess references in his plays, by which he counts any chess terms, which obviously also have much wider uses, such as knight, bishop, queen and draw. Surely even Wall cannot believe that Richard III's, "A horse! A horse! My kingdom for a horse!" (*Richard III*) is chess-related?

With rather more basis in fact, Wall gives biographies of numerous famous players, including the world champions, along with Anderssen, Staunton and Boleslavsky, whilst there is some interesting historical reading, especially on religion and chess. Surfers may well find something of amusement here, be it with Beavis and Butthead in 'The Chess Lecture', or from new chess titles, such as *My Worst Games* by Alexander Alekwine, devised by Wall himself. There is also plenty of trivia with which to impress friends.

2) The Bobby Fischer Home Page **
www.rio.com/~johnnymc

Headers: *Results, 732 games, Best 100, Opponents, Opening repertoire, Openings index, ECO index, Endgame index, Photos, ECO openings, Chess quotes, Author info*

A Fischer enthusiast called Johnny McMenamin is responsible for this patchy site. Not all the information fits on the screen, and whilst there are indexes of the 732 games available, these only refer to game numbers and there are no hyperlinks to displaying the games themselves. The games available, and only 60 of the best 100 are, can only be viewed in text form anyway. That said, there are some interesting articles on Fischer, including one written during the Yugoslavia Fischer-Spassky rematch by Ivan Solotaroff, whilst there are also many good photos. Surfers are promised "the complete set of Fischer radio interviews" and what Bobby has been up to since 1992. However, since these promises were made back in the summer of 1999, it is likely that these features, which would interest all Fischer fans, may well not materialise.

3) The Chess Café *****
www.chesscafe.com

Headers: *What's New, Tournament World, Columns, Bulletin Board, Bookstore & Emporium, Book Reviews, Skittles Room, Endgame Studies, Archives*

Pricecheck: *Polished Natural and Ebonized Boxwood Chess Set US$139.00 plus $8.34 shipping (North America) /$16.68 (Europe),* Play the Open Games as Black *$22.95 plus $5.95 shipping (North America) /$11.90 (Europe), Chess Assistant 5.0 + Ultimate Game Collection 4 $129.95 plus $7.80 (North America) /$15.59 (Europe)*

The Chess Café is arguably the highest quality chess website around: articles by some of the world's leading chess writers are beautifully presented with diagrams and photographs, and there is something new to read on every visit. The columns are a sumptuous feast—they are all excellent, with something to interest everyone. Tony Miles provides the viewpoint of a professional player, especially with regard to chess politics; whilst Gary Lane sorts out opening questions, and international arbiter, Geurt Gijssen, clearly answers readers' queries about the bizarre rules dilemmas they are taxed by. These and all the other columnists write clearly, enthusiastically and often humorously, and if you can't wait to read the latest columns, then it is possible to sign-up to an e-mail list, which provides a weekly update of what is new on the site.

The book reviews are more thorough than those of most publications, whilst Carsten Hansen, in his separate column, 'Checkpoint', also devoted to reviews, challenges authors' analysis. Hansen also reviews magazines, something which is not too common elsewhere, and readers will quickly learn which books are a waste of money. You can purchase books, along with other chess items, from the Bookstore and Emporium, which is easy to navigate and has a good search facility. New tournaments are advertised free on Tournament World, whilst readers can have their say or ask questions on the Bulletin Board. This has seen debate about whether Morphy had a gay lover; issues can get fairly personal once historians Ken Whyld, Edward Winter and Louis Blair become involved.

The Chess Café's collection of historical material is unparalleled on the Internet, including such gems as Alexander Alekhine letters; an 1859 article about the Boston banquet in honour of Paul Morphy; and Bobby Fischer's article, 'A Bust to the King's Gambit'. History is often dealt with in Tim Harding's 'The Kibitzer' column, whilst Hanon Russell must be praised for recruiting Swiss IM Richard Forster as a columnist, and allowing him to pursue his love of chess history. If you miss a column, it could not be easier to locate it in the Archives section, which also allows you to search through all the columns that have ever appeared on this site for any topic. For both the chess historian, and indeed any chess player surfing the web, the Chess Café cannot be missed.

4) Chess on Stamps *****
www.tri.org.au/chess
Headers: *Gallery, Online Catalogue*

Pricecheck: *Set of five Yugoslav stamps (1950) commemorating the Dubrovnik Olympiad US$30.00, One Great Britain stamp (1976) of a Caxton woodcut $1.50*

Dr Colin Rose, an Australian economist/mathematician and philatelist (co-author of many academic treatises, including *Sharks, Speculative Attack and the Hump-Shaped Distribution*), has produced an elegant site with an extensive catalogue of stamps for collectors and a gallery for the casual visitor. Virtually all stamps in the collection, produced between 1947 and 1990, are displayed. To be in it, they must be considered legitimate stamps, which eliminates many emanating from ex-USSR states. Interestingly, Capablanca features on 37 stamps; Karpov, perhaps fittingly given his interest in philately, on 24; and then there is quite a drop to Kasparov, who features on 10. Should you gain an interest in chess philately from this site, there are comprehensive lists and links to societies and catalogues devoted to this hobby.

5) The Game is Afoot *
www.pstat.ucsb.edu/~carlson/chess
Headers: *Archives, Biographies*

This site features biographies of Tal, Philidor, Morphy, Tarrasch, Lasker, Pillsbury, Rubinstein, Nimzowitsch, Capablanca, Réti, Alekhine, Najdorf, Reshevsky and Sultan Khan by Terry Crandall. Apparently, more are available in the archives section, but only if site designer Claudia Carlson turns the 'Archives' header into a hyperlink to the archives page, assuming the page actually exists. The biographies themselves do not feature any new information and are fairly short. Crandall sometimes adds a personal viewpoint, such as for Tal, whom he once met, whilst there are brief descriptions of players' styles and sometimes critics' views on them, as well as a short biography. There are also a few photos and sketches, but no games, so for information on any of these players, you are better off with a standard published work on them.

6) On Nimzowitsch ***
www.xs4all.nl/~wimnij/bio.html

Headers: *Why these notes and abstracts?*, *Biographical Outlines*, *The match Nimzowitsch-Aljechin*, *Nimzowitsch' esthetic credo*, *Cultural Crosslinks*, *Some reactions I received about "On Nimzowitsch"*, *Nimzocircle*

This site contains some interesting material on certain aspects of Nimzowitsch's life. There are many extracts from historical works on the turbulent political situation in Riga shortly after the First World War, which may well explain why Nimzowitsch moved to Copenhagen from Riga in 1920. Under 'Nimzowitsch' esthetic credo', the site's author, Willem Jan Nijenhuis, provides some thought-provoking views on some of Nimzowitsch's ideas, whilst he also contrasts Nimzowitsch with Joyce's protagonist in *Portrait of the Artist as a Young Man*. The highbrow discussion continues in 'Cultural Crosslinks', but fortunately all the lengthy quotations used, bar one in German, are in English.

The main highlight of the site, for those not too interested in Nimzowitsch's views and life, is being able to play through all 21 games between Nimzowitsch and Alekhine using Java, or downloading them in PGN. There is a good selection of links to other sites featuring Nimzowitsch, and if you like what you see here, you can subscribe to an e-mail group, NimzoCircle.

6
Archives
& Databases

Whether you are a professional player who needs to see the latest games of Kasparov and Kramnik, or a chess enthusiast in search of 19th-century double rook sacrifices, the Internet is a fantastic resource. Thousands of games can be downloaded in minutes, with the help of some important tools. You'll need a free program such as WinZip or PKZip to unzip large files, and preferably ChessBase or the free version, ChessBase Light, for viewing the games. Many of these sites, however, offer more than just games—there are photographs, player biographies and articles, too. In this chapter, there is a proliferation of five-star sites, reflecting the amount of effort which some Webmasters are putting in, usually as a hobby.

A/ Webmaster Hall of Fame
Mark Orr, The Irish Chess Archive

Please introduce yourself

I'm 45, married, one child (a 14-year-old daughter). I work as a senior Web developer in a .com company and obtained this position as a direct consequence of the experience gained while developing the Irish Chess Archive. Previously, I was a research scientist in statistics, robotics and radio astronomy. The common link between all of them is computers. Although born and brought up in Northern Ireland; at 18, I moved to Edinburgh to attend university and, apart from a few years in Manchester, have been there ever since.

My Dad taught my brother and I chess when we were both still young. He promised a pound for the first one to beat him. My brother won the pound and I was so upset, my Dad let me beat him and gave me a pound too. Nearly 40 years later, here I am still trying to prove something, while my brother never took chess seriously.

In 1983 I got an IM norm out of the blue (I hardly knew what an IM norm was), playing in a tournament in Italy. Five years later I got two more norms just before the deadline on the first one ran out, and thus became Ireland's first IM. I won the Irish Championship in 1985 and 1994 and, apart from 1998, when my wife was ill, I've played for Ireland in all the Olympiads since 1984.

How often do you have a chance to play chess and do you wish you could play more?

Not very often. Mainly Olympiads; Kilkenny and Bunratty in Ireland; the occasional Irish Championship; the occasional weekend tournament in Scotland; and training games with local players in Edinburgh, usually on a weekday evening after work. It's very tiring, but it's better than nothing. When I was younger, I used to play in Hastings every year, which I loved, but I haven't been there since the mid-eighties. I just don't have time; I wish I did. Basically, I need to win the lottery so I can give up work.

Do you play chess on the Internet—if so, where?

The Internet Chess Club—where else? I must say I find the standard quite high. I can't get above 2200 at speed chess, although that's never been my forte anyway. However, I find the absence of an opponent actually sitting there on the other side of the board, takes away a lot of the excitement of the game.

When and why did you decide to set up a Website?

It all started in 1994 when I overheard a couple of old fogies at an Irish Championship talking about a well-known Irish player from the past whom they had known when he was alive. I realised I knew nothing about this man, nor about many of the other 'great' (relatively speaking!) Irish players, and it would be interesting to find out more. I had an idea that researching a person's life and, in particular, how chess had fitted into it, would be both interesting, and potentially rewarding, in regard to the lessons one might learn.

For example, one question which I hoped to be able to shed some light on, was why do so many of Ireland's talented players reach a certain standard (around IM) and then give up the game? I know there's an obvious answer to this question (work and family), but not everyone who has to work and support a family gives up chess entirely. Why did Kernan, Dunne, the Delaney brothers, Moles, MacGrillen, Henry, Cronin and others feel it necessary to pack the game in and does the same fate await Kelly, Heidenfeld and Quinn when they reach their late 20s or early 30s?

Initially I thought of a book, but it wasn't long before my interest in computers propelled me into setting up a Website instead. Besides, books are like stone—once written, they can't be changed. Websites can be continuously updated (but, on the other hand, need someone to take responsibility for their maintenance). Another change to the original idea is that the site has become a repository for all kinds of historical records about Irish chess, not just the player profiles. Since it's concerned with Irish chess and oriented towards the past, I decided to call it, 'The Irish Chess Archive', or TICA for short.

In March 2000 TICA moved to a new address, why was that?

The old Website was hosted on computers belonging to the same academic research group for which I worked and I had the luxury of being able to control the Web server set-up. When I changed jobs (October 1999) the site remained there for a while, but of course I had to move it eventually. That's when reality kicked in...

Did you have any technical problems?

Initially basically no, although I was helped in this regard by being able to use my work computers to serve the Website, so it didn't cost me anything and I had a say in how the server program was configured. I prepared the Web pages on my Windows95 PC at home and downloaded them to the Unix computers at work. The data for the site (results, profiles, ratings and so on) is kept in a collection of plain text files. A set of Perl scripts, run from a graphical interface, maintain these data files and write the Web pages from them. Using programs, rather than doing it by hand, helps avoid problems with broken links and inconsistencies, makes it possible to implement site-wide changes at a stroke and saves a lot of time in the long run.

My fear that problems would arise when I moved to a commercial ISP proved well founded. I moved the site early in 2000 to an ISP called Global Internet (*www.globalnet.co.uk*), for which I paid £200 in advance for a year's Internet access and the Web hosting services, including a new domain name. Everything worked fine except the one CGI script I have on my site, a program written in the Perl programming language. The script draws graphs of players' rating history in response to a user clicking on buttons on a form.

I found out that the problem was caused by the fact that a non-standard but popular extension to Perl, which my script uses, was not installed on Global Internet's server. However, I was not unduly concerned by this as I had anticipated this problem, and before I joined, had specifically confirmed with a Global representative that missing Perl modules could be installed if required. So I contacted Global asking them to install the required bit of Perl code, a job which literally takes about 30 seconds for someone who knows what they're doing. That's when I learnt my first hard lesson.

Over the coming weeks I learnt just how frustrating dealing with someone who is only interested in getting your money and holding on to it can be. Their position can be summed up by: Sorry sir, our policy is not to install non-standard Perl modules. Sorry sir, our technical team will not reconsider your request. Sorry sir, you cannot have shell access to your Website to install it yourself. Sorry sir, we cannot refund your subscription.

Disgruntled, I couldn't stomach staying with this ISP so I moved again, this time to a local ISP in Edinburgh (*www.ednet.co.uk*), and forked out another £200. I had a long face-to-face chat with them about Perl modules before I joined, as you can imagine, and I'm glad to report I've had no problems.

What material can people find on your site that they can't find in magazines and books?

There are no publicly available records in any form devoted exclusively to Irish chess, certainly none are kept by the Irish Chess Union. Of course Irish players do get occasional mentions in chess magazines and Irish chess gets some coverage in books on chess in general, but nowhere else is so much information brought together under one roof. Let me stress I'm talking mainly about historical data here. *The Irish*

Chess Journal and the Website, 'Chess Ireland', do a good job, covering the contemporary scene.

Since I still play on the Irish team, when I go abroad to European team championships and Olympiads, I can report back to the Website almost in real time. See my Batumi report (*www.markorr.net/tica/teams/reports/batumi99.html*), which contains a diary as well as results and pictures taken with a digital camera.

Where do you get your material from? Is there anything you wouldn't publish, e.g. because it was too controversial?

The players' profiles I usually get by asking people to make contributions, or sometimes by interviewing players or using interviews conducted and published elsewhere. For players who have long since gone up to the great tournament in the sky, I rely on newspaper obituaries, descriptions from relatives or fellow players and material in old chess magazines.

The other data (games, records, pictures and so on) I get from a variety of sources: chess magazines, tournament booklets, newspapers, private collections and so on. Many of the pictures of contemporary players I take myself, which explains why I'm often to be seen skulking around with a camera at Irish chess tournaments.

Here I must mention the work of David McAlister. Shortly after I put the site online David, who lives in Northern Ireland, began e-mailing me with corrections and new information for the site. Soon he began sending quite substantial pieces of research, which were the fruits of long hours spent in his local library. His contributions have been invaluable and I'm very grateful for his continued support. To begin with, he sent me quite a lot of the very historical stuff (I'm talking the century before last!), which he's more interested in than I am, but his contributions have tailed off recently (he now has other responsibilities, like being President of the ICU).

Obviously, some of the material I get on some players can be quite fascinating, but a little too hot for publication. Things like opinions on their sexual preferences or stories about their bad behaviour. It could be argued that everything is relevant to understanding someone's life and should therefore be included. That may be true, but there are degrees of relevance (especially since the focus here is mainly on chess) and a potentially high price to be paid defending the inclusion of controversial or sensitive material. Don't get me wrong, I love it when someone tells me some juicy gossip, but as for actually using it in the site, my instinct, as in chess, is to avoid murky complications unless absolutely necessary.

Do you pay contributors and do you worry about copyright issues, i.e. whether it's OK to publish something or whether people will copy things from your site?

No, I certainly can't afford to pay contributors. If the site was commercially sponsored that might be possible, but with its specialist subject matter, it doesn't attract enough 'hits' to be attractive to advertisers. Perhaps if I can persuade players to pose nude...

If I want to use substantial parts of a published article for the site (as in the case of the material on Brian Reilly, late editor of the *British Chess Magazine*) I ask permission first, and then, assuming it's granted, acknowledge the source. As for people copying stuff from TICA, copying games and bits of the records is fine, but I think it would be appropriate to acknowledge the source if people want to republish substantial parts. If something David or I had put a lot of work into (say, the entire Irish Championship record or a profile of some player from the past) was copied and published without acknowledgment, I'd be annoyed (though there isn't much we could do about it).

How much time do you spend working on your site?

When I was writing the software to maintain it, my wife regarded herself as a TICA widow. After that, not so much—maybe about an hour per day on average, depending on what new material happened to come in. However, during the Elista Olympiad I probably did at least three hours per day. Nowadays not so much, except in short tremendous bursts. My main problem is getting material from players. You may notice on the site that some contemporary players have a profile while others don't. I've tracked down those that don't and asked them to contribute their story. Generally they say they would be delighted and then I wait and wait and nothing happens. Then when I contact them again they apologise for the delay and we discuss what they're going to write about and they promise to get onto it very soon and then I wait and wait and still nothing happens.

One of the worst offenders in this regard is Paul Delaney, who I really thought was going to pull out his finger at last after I had a long chat with him in Bunratty, early in 1999—I've not heard from him since. I don't know what to do about this problem. Most people would just give up, but I don't like to admit defeat. I shall probably end up being extremely rude to someone, which, although it will give me tremendous satisfaction, will bring to an abrupt end any remaining chances of getting anything from them.

Have you spent money on it or is it just time?

Initially mainly just time, unless you include some of the books on things like HTML, Perl and JavaScript, which I might have bought anyway. Then I bought an old evil ISP (Global

Internet) for £200, a new lovely ISP (*www.ednet.co.uk*) also for £200, and a digital camera for £300.

How much feedback do you get from visitors to your site and what are their main criticisms/aspects that they particularly like?

Very little feedback of any kind. Sometimes other Webmasters compliment me on my site, which is most gratifying, so I say nice things back to them about theirs. Maybe that's the only positive feedback we get, from each other. If it weren't for the server's log files of hits, which are reassuringly full, I would hardly know anyone was using the site at all. From time to time, people offer information for the site, which is nice. I have a page acknowledging all the people who have ever helped, even if it's just in small ways. All I can say is that it's just like real life. We all take things for granted and never stop to think who created the things we use and how much work they put in to create them.

What has been your greatest scoop?

This used to be my coverage of the Elista Olympiad. I had been due to play for Ireland, but my wife was ill on the morning of departure and I missed the plane. I was very disappointed and couldn't bear going back to work, so I threw myself into covering the Olympiad on TICA. I monitored the raw games as they were relayed by a Website in Russia and posted the main and Irish results to TICA, plus some commentary, as quickly as I could. It was "near live coverage", as described later by another Webmaster. Also, as luck would have it, the last day of the Olympiad was on a Monday and so, still officially on leave to play, I stayed home and finished a report of the event. Many of the other Webmasters had to go to work and I got out the final results almost 24 hours before most of the other amateur sites.

The coverage of the Batumi 1999 European Championships was, however, even better, because: (a) I was there; (b) I managed to find time to report every evening; and (c) I had a digital camera with me.

Was it easy to update TICA with live reports from the 1999 European Team Championship in Georgia?

No. The press centre at the playing venue was slow to get its Internet act together. But with the help of our team's interpreter, I found a student centre in town with an Internet connection. For every round except the last (when the press centre finally got organised), I would retire to my hotel room in the evening and prepare the update to TICA on my laptop.

Then in the morning I would go into town to the student centre with the update on a floppy disk and borrow someone's computer long enough to send the file back to the Web server. All this was complicated by our bad-tempered team bus driver who didn't like getting up early in the morning and the frequent power cuts which are the norm in Georgia. Also, all this Website stuff took time away from socialising with other players in the evening and preparation for the games in the morning. So next time I'll try not to spend so much time on it.

What are your future plans for the site?

Of some concern to me is what will happen to the site after I am gone. Hopefully this counts as long-term planning, but I'd like to think that what I've started will be carried on somehow, and not just be something that's here today and gone tomorrow. I'm not sure what to do about this, but one hare-brained idea is... What if the site was not controlled by a human Webmaster, but by a software robot (e.g. a Perl program), which negotiates new additions to the site from anyone who wants to contribute.

Some prototype programs like this exist already, but are not yet sophisticated enough. The idea goes something like this: suppose someone wanted to submit the results of the Irish Championships to the site. They would prepare the results in a plain text file in some reasonable format and e-mail them to the robot or tell it (via a Web interface) at what URL it could pick up the data. The robot would then inspect what was being submitted to the site, check it out, make sure it's consistent and then either accept it and include it in the site, or query it, pointing out the inconsistencies or ambiguities and inviting the contributor to correct these before resending it.

This would solve the problem of keeping the site going after I'm gone but raise other issues, security being the obvious one. You might say it would be easier just to find a someone else to take over from me, but I worry: will he or she love and cherish this site as much as I do? A robot, I could build in my own image, then I would live forever! Well, maybe I'm getting a bit carried away with this idea. I also have some great ideas for nicely displaying chess games, while still allowing them to be interactive. The problem with all this is finding the time. As a full time Web professional now, all my energies go into the Website at work, leaving me precious little for TICA when I get home.

Which Websites are your own personal favourites, and which do you consider to be rivals?

The Week In Chess is the site I visit most. I download games from TWIC and rely on it for links to sites of current interest (e.g. if there's a big tournament going on somewhere). After that, the FIDE site for ratings and FIDE news, BritBase for more games, and Chess Ireland for what's happening in Irish chess. Chess Ireland concentrates on current Irish chess, whereas TICA is mainly focused on the past, so I regard the two sites as complementing each other rather than as rivals.

One new Irish site, which recently came online describing itself as the 'official' Irish Website, contained no links to or mention of TICA whatsoever. Somewhat indignant, I politely pointed out the omission to the person behind the site but, once again, though a promise was made, the goods were not delivered. Much to my satisfaction, this site remains to this day, what it started out as: badly designed, and rife with broken links and scripts! (That doesn't sound too bitter, does it?)

B/ Best of the Web

Keres plays with the Wehrmacht

by Tomasz Lissowski

Contrary to the Latin saying that, "During war, the Muses are silent," Caissa was not mute during World War II. The game of chess, with its dual nature of sport and pastime, and of course, because of its close association with images of military conquest and war, became a small but active component of the Wheels of War on both sides. The German command, following Dr. Goebbels' slogan, "All forces—for the front," included chess in its programme called 'Truppenbetreuung' or 'Pastimes for soldiers'. Groups of chess masters circulated from field hospitals to barracks to mess halls, playing exhibition tournaments and giving simultaneous displays.

In May 1943, after Wehrmacht troops had disastrously lost the Battle of Stalingrad, a 'Truppenbetreuung' event was held by the occupying authorities in the Polish city of Poznan. In November 1939, the Germans had renamed that unfortunate city 'Posen', directly annexing the city and its captive people into the Reich. The main attraction for the audience at the event would be the presence of Paul Keres, the Estonian grandmaster, a player generally recognized since AVRO 1938, as a candidate for the world chess championship.

The war's destiny for Keres (1916-1975) and his small homeland was one of bitter restraint and difficult circumstance. In recalling the forgotten Poznan episode from the chess career of this splendid sportsman and individual, whose portrait was placed on bank notes in 1991, by a newly independent Estonia, I will refrain from political or ethical conclusions and, instead, focus strictly on the facts. Most of the reports which follow are generally unknown in chess circles, as is the accompanying photograph of a young Keres. These were found in the annals of *Ostdeutscher Beobachter*, the German newspaper issued in occupied Poznan. These reports, it should be emphasized, would have been almost impossible to locate without the kind guidance and suggestion of Professor Andrzej Kwilecki, the leading expert on Poznan chess history.

An anonymous journalist reported the following to his readers on Monday, May 24, 1943:

"The Days of Chess for Wehrmacht in Posen began Sunday afternoon with a short ceremony in the Great Hall of Reichsuniversitat *[before and after the war known as Adam Mickiewicz University—T.L.]*. Afterwards, simultaneous exhibitions were conducted, with the participation of the world championship candidate Paul Keres (Reval) against forty players; and three chess masters: Eysser (Bayreuth), Rogmann (Berlin) and Dr. Kraemer (Posen), each against twenty opponents, mostly soldiers.

The opening ceremonies of this, the hitherto largest chess event for the Wehrmacht in the District of Varta River, was attended by representatives of the Wehrmacht, the State, and the Party, with General Bielfeld, military commandant in Posen, among the honorable visitors.

"In his short speech, party comrade Dr. Altmann, who was representing the German Labor Front for the Management of Varta District, expressed his joy at the large attendance at a chess event organized by the National—Socialistic Commune 'Kraft durch Freude' *['Force through Joy', a Nazi governmental agency organizing holidays and other events for Reich employees—T.L.]* in cooperation with the All-German Chess Union, on behalf of the Wehrmacht Main Headquarters, for purposes of the military forces' recreation chess program. The speaker announced that District Management had established a special prize. Military commandant, General Bielfeld, in the name of all the soldiers who were taking part in the event, thanked the organizers for setting up the exhibition. The General noted that chess play requires certain features, which could be said to be truly soldierly in nature: courage, concentration, logical thinking and ambition. Wehrmacht Command will accordingly continue to promote chess among its soldiers as one of the more useful pastimes.

"Reichsschachwart *[Reich Chess Secretary—T.L.]* Majer described the actions undertaken by "Kraft und Freude" for placing chess (a game unlike any other and one involving numerous features of character and intellect, ones particularly useful for developing the spirit) on such a wide basis for the people. Chess was a very popular source of diversion and relaxation among soldiers between battles, as well as at field hospitals, during the First World War. In the same manner, chess is a useful military amusement during the present war. Comrade Majer then introduced the world championship candidate, Paul Keres, who during the past seven years has successfully participated in international tournaments, reaching a place in the first rank of internationally known chess masters.

"The Secretary also introduced the other chess masters present in Posen, namely Gruenfeld (Vienna), Rogmann (Berlin), Eysser (Bayreuth) and also Obergefreite Bickenbach (Posen) *[Obergefreite ranks between a Private and a Corporal—T.L.]*, who jointly with Keres will take part in a four day encounter starting on the following Monday in Posener Hoff *[Poznan Castle—T.L.]*, wishing them both luck for a hopefully fascinating event.

"Afterwards, four masters approached the boards for simultaneous play. The largest interest, of course, focused on the forty games conducted by Grandmaster Keres. Though the boards where Rogmann, Eysser and Dr. Kraemer were playing against twenty each, however, were also besieged by kibitzers. After only a few minutes Rogmann gained the first victory, when one of his antagonists resigned in a lost position. Shortly thereafter, Keres won his first point too, though he faced twice the number of opponents. As time went on, numerous players were dispatched, until finally only the hardiest and most implacable players withstood the master's superior knowledge.

"The display ended after slightly more than four hours. According to expectations, Keres came off as the grand victor with 33½-6½. He won 32 games, drew 3, and lost 5. Rogmann won 15 games, drew 3, and lost 2 (scoring a total of 16½-3½). Eysser won 17, drew one, and lost two times (scoring 17½-2½). Dr. Kraemer defeated 16 partners, played one draw, and had to reconcile himself to 3 defeats (scoring 16½-3½).

"The following players finished their games against Keres successfully: Sonderfuehrer Waeber, Sonderfuehrer Lau, Barthell, Jannasch, Popp (Reich's Railway); draws were made by Oberfeldfebel Biedendorf, Gefreite Bruechold, and Gefreite Kanitz. Against Rogmann, Lieutenant Braun and Gefreite Maier won; Thuernau, Wachmeister Zwergel and Oberfeldfebel Junker played a draw. Eysser was defeated by Rueffer (Reich's Railway) and Gefreite Waldheuer, with a draw reached by Sturm. The victory over Dr. Kraemer were gained by Oberarzt Dr. Thomas Hauptmann of Schutzpolizei, Roelofsen and Unteroffizier Winnerling, Poppenberg played a draw. Sonderfuehrer Waeber gained the XXI Military Region prize for the first victory over Keres."

Ostdeutscher Beobachter, 1943.05.24

KERES, GRUENFELD, ROGMANN WIN
The First Round of the Master Chess Tournament

The first round of the Posen Chess Master Tournament for the Wehrmacht was played on Monday. The main interest centered on the game of the world chess championship candidate Keres with Obergefreite Bickenbach. In the endgame, Keres won without incident, despite his opponent's obstinate resistance. In the game between Master Eysser from Bayreuth and Rogmann, the latter remained victorious after he weakened his opponent's queenside by a surprising tactical manoeuvre. In the game Gruenfeld versus Kieninger, Gruenfeld slowly and carefully built an advantage, winning the game due to his passed pawn. Keres, Gruenfeld and Rogmann now lead.

Ostdeutscher Beobachter, 1943.05.25

Bickenbach *White*
P.Keres *Black*
Poznan, 24 May 1943
Two Knights Defence

1 e4 e5 2 ♘f3 ♘c6 3 ♗c4 ♘f6 4 ♘c3 ♘xe4 5 ♘xe4 d5 6 ♗xd5 ♕xd5 7 ♘c3 ♕a5 8 d3 ♗g4 9 ♗d2 ♘d4 10 ♘e2 ♘xf3+ 11 gxf3 ♕d5 12 ♘c3 ♕xf3 13 ♕xf3 ♗xf3 14 ♖g1 0-0-0 15 ♖g3 ♗c6 16 0-0-0 ♖d4 17 ♖e1 ♖h4 18 h3 f5 19 ♖g5 g6 20 ♖xe5 ♖xh3 21 ♖g1 ♗d6 22 ♖e2 ♗f3 23 ♖e6 ♔d7 24 ♖ge1 a6 25 ♗g5 h6 26 ♗f6 ♖g8 27 a3 g5 28 b4 ♖g6 29 d4 ♖h1 30 ♖xh1 ♔xe6 0-1

Paul Keres: Photographs and Games, Tallinn 1995, p158

SECOND ROUND
Keres and Rogmann Lead

In the second round of the masters' tournament for the Wehrmacht in 'Posener Hoff', tense and complicated games developed. In a Spanish Opening, the world championship candidate Keres, proposed to Vienna chess master Gruenfeld the exchange of queens, in order to maintain a small but lasting pressure. Gruenfeld held out for a draw, but after he made several imprudent moves, Keres' rooks invaded the kingside. Gruenfeld overstepped the time limit in a lost position. A Spanish Opening between Rogmann and Kieninger was adjourned after 40 moves, but on resumption was easily won by Rogmann. A wonderful success was gained by Obergefreite Bickenbach against Bayreuth master Eysser. The game ended in a draw. The score after the second round: Keres and Rogmann—2 points each,

Gruenfeld—1 point, Obergefreite Bickenbach and Eysser—½ point each, Kieninger—0 points.

Some valuable awards for the master tournament have been offered by the mayor of Posen, as well as by the Wehrmacht Commandant and the Regional Management of the German Labor Front. In addition, the Posen Commune of 'Force through Joy' has offered a brilliancy prize.

P.Keres *White*
E.Gruenfeld *Black*
Poznan, 24 May 1943
Spanish: Closed (Knight Attack)
(Annotations by G.R. in *Deutsche Schachzeitung*)

1 e4 e5 2 ♘f3 ♘c6 3 ♗b5 a6 4 ♗a4 ♘f6 5 0-0 ♗e7 6 ♘c3 b5 7 ♗b3 d6 8 ♘d5 ♘a5 9 ♘xe7 ♕xe7 10 d4 ♘xb3 11 axb3 ♗b7

11...♗g4 was a serious alternative; on b7 the bishop doesn't play a large role.

12 ♗g5 h6 13 ♗xf6 ♕xf6 14 ♖e1 0-0 15 dxe5 dxe5 16 ♕d3

Now, and in the future, the break ...c7-c5 must be avoided.

16...♖fe8 17 ♕c3 ♕e7 18 b4 ♖ac8 19 ♕c5

The break ...c7-c5 must be prevented at any price. After queens are exchanged White preserves some pressure.

19...♕xc5 20 bxc5 ♖cd8 21 ♖e2 ♖e7 22 ♘e1 f6 23 f3 ♖ed7 24 ♘d3 ♖d4 25 ♔f2 ♖a8 26 ♖a5 ♔f7 27 ♔e3 ♖ad8 28 ♖d2 ♔e7 29 g4 ♗c8

Something should have been done against the opponent's threatened action on the kingside; 29...h5 was officious.

30 ♖a1 ♗b7 31 h4 g5?

Now White's rooks will invade through the h-file into Black's position.

32 hxg5 hxg5 33 ♖h1 ♖f8

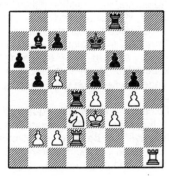

34 c3!
A quiet but powerful move.
34...♖a4

Returning to d7 would have been an error for 35 ♖h7+ ♖f7 36 ♖xf7+ ♔xf7 37 ♘xe5+.

35 ♖h7+ ♖f7 36 ♖dh2 ♗c8 37 ♖xf7+ ♔xf7 38 ♖h7+ ♔g6 39 ♖xc7 ♗e6 40 ♖c6

And in this hopeless position Black overstepped the time limit.

1-0 (Time).

Deutsche Schachzeitung 1943, p.62
Paul Keres: Photographs and Games, Tallinn 1995, p158

KERES IN FIRST PLACE
Rogmann Delivers a Dramatic Game to Keres

In the third round of the Posen Masters' Chess Tournament for the Wehrmacht, Gruenfeld won against Eysser who in the middlegame did not find the best defense. Rogmann secured a point in the game against Obergefreite Bickenbach. Kieninger held an isolated central pawn against Keres. This weakness ran through the whole game as a red thread. Nevertheless Kieninger defended obstinately. The game was adjourned and will be continued today. After three rounds Keres and Rogmann lead with 3 points, followed by Gruenfeld with 2 points. *[Keres' score seems like speculation as his adjourned game had yet to be finished.- T.L.]*

The fourth round saw the dramatic game between Rogmann and Keres. In the Spanish Opening, Rogmann gained a wonderful attacking position. It appeared Keres was about to lose, but then he found a defense. In an interesting position, Rogmann had a sure draw in hand. Still, he wanted to win, and fell victim in his attempt after a surprising retort by his opponent. Rogmann resigned to Keres after four hours. Gruenfeld defended against Bickenbach *à la* Prussian. He won the endgame after hard resistance. The game Eysser-Kieninger was adjourned in a position difficult to evaluate.

Keres played his fifth round and final game a day early against Eysser. He forced the Bayreuth master to resign after thirty moves. Thus with four points, Keres secured first place in the tournament. A hard fight between Gruenfeld and Rogmann is expected today on 1 o'clock, PM, until 5 o'clock. The game Kieninger-Bickenbach will decide who will be fourth in this tournament.

Tonight at 8 o'clock, a farewell banquet will be held in the 'Posener Hoff', together with the award ceremony for the tournament winner. It will be held in collaboration with the Reich Theater of Posen *[Wielki Theater—T.L.]*. Soldiers and civilians interested in chess are invited.

Ostdeutscher Beobachter, 1943.05.27

G.Kieninger *White*
P.Keres *Black*
Poznan, 25 May 1925
Semi-Slav: Exchange

1 d4 ♘f6 2 c4 e6 3 ♘f3 d5 4 ♘c3 c6 5 e3 ♘bd7 6 cxd5 exd5 7 ♗d3 ♗d6 8 0-0 0-0 9 ♖e1 ♖e8 10 ♕c2 ♘f8 11 e4 dxe4 12 ♘xe4 ♘d5 13 ♗g5 f6 14 ♘xd6 ♖xe1+ 15 ♖xe1 ♕xd6 16 ♗h4 ♗e6 17 ♗g3 ♕d7 18 a3 ♘b6 19 ♕c5 ♖d8 20 h3 ♘c8 21 ♗e4 a6 22 ♕b4 ♘e7 23 ♗b1 ♘fg6 24 h4 ♗g4 25 ♗a2+ ♘d5 26 ♘h2 ♗e6 27 ♕d2 ♘f8 28 ♕a5 ♗f7 29 ♘f3 ♘e7 30 ♗xf7+ ♔xf7 31 ♗c7 ♖e8 32 ♗b6 ♘d5 33 ♖xe8 ♕xe8 34 ♗c5 ♘g6 35 h5 ♘gf4 36 ♘h4 ♕d7 37 h6 g5 38 ♘f3 ♘xg2 39 ♔xg2 ♕g4+ 40 ♔h2 ♕xf3 41 ♕d8 ♕xf2+ 42 ♔h1 ♕e1+ 43 ♔h2 ♘f4 44 ♕f8+ ♔g6 45 ♕g7+ ♔h5 46 ♕xh7 ♕f2+ 47 ♔h1 ♕g2 mate. 0-1

Paul Keres: Photographs and Games, Tallinn 1995, p158

G.Rogmann *White*
Paul Keres *Black*
Poznan, 26 May 1943
Spanish: Closed (Center Attack)
(Annotations by G.R. in *Deutsche Schachzeitung*)

1 e4 e5 2 ♘f3 ♘c6 3 ♗b5 a6 4 ♗a4 ♘f6 5 0-0 ♗e7 6 d4 exd4 7 e5 ♘e4 8 ♖e1 ♘c5 9 ♗xc6 dxc6 10 ♘xd4 0-0
Gruenfeld and other masters prefer 10...♘e6 and, as shown by this game, that line seems to be better.
11 ♘c3 ♖e8 12 ♗e3 ♗f8 13 f4 f6 14 exf6 ♕xf6
The same move was played by P.Keres against Dr Alekhine in Kemeri 1937. That game, which ended in a draw, was unknown to the commander of the white forces.
15 ♕f3 ♗f5
Surprising because Black in this line tries to preserve his pair of bishops as compensation for White's better pawn position. In this sense 15...♗d7 comes into account.
16 ♘xf5 ♕xf5 17 ♖e2 h5
This weakening move is hard to avoid, as g2-g4 is a permanent threat. White's position is indoubtedly superior, moreover Black must avoid a general exchange in order not to lose the endgame.
18 ♖ae1 ♖ad8
18...♗d6 immediately was better. Now Black's position becomes critical.
19 ♔f1! ♗d6 20 ♗xc5 ♖xe2 21 ♕xe2! ♕xc5
Forced; if 21...♗xc5, 22 ♕c4+ followed by 23 ♖e5 and the bishop is lost.
22 ♕e6+ ♔h8

23 ♘e4

In preliminary calculations, White planned to play 23 ♕f7, then later the seemingly strong knight move.

23...♕xc2!

The saving idea! The endgame after 23...♕d5 24 ♕xd5 cxd5 25 ♘xd6 ♖xd6 26 ♖e7 would be inconvenient for Black.

24 ♘g5

White seemingly had a win in his pocket, threatening 25 ♘f7+, as well as 25 ♕e8+. However, the open position of White's king allows Keres to slip away.

24...♕d3+! 25 ♔g1?

White plays carelessly for a win and overlooks a nice rejoinder. 25 ♖e2 would have been better, after which Black should have taken the draw by perpetual check.

25...♕d4+ 26 ♔h1 ♕xf4

The refutation!

27 ♘f7+ ♔h7 28 ♘xd6 ♖xd6 29 ♕e8 ♕f5 30 h3 ♖d2 31 ♕b8 ♕d5 32 ♖g1 ♖xb2 33 ♕xc7 c5 34 a4 c4 35 ♕g3 ♕e4 36 ♖e1 h4 37 ♕xg7+ ♔xg7 38 ♖xe4 c3 39 ♖c4 c2 40 ♔h2 b5 41 axb5 axb5 42 ♖c7+ ♔f6

After a few moves White resigned.

43 ♖c6+ ♔e5 44 ♖c5+ ♔d4 45 ♖h5 c1=♕ 46 ♖d5+ ♔e3 47 ♖d3+ ♔e2 0-1

Deutsche Schachzeitung 1943, p.62-63
Paul Keres: Photographs and Games, Tallinn 1995,
p158-159

GRUENFELD SECOND PRIZE-WINNER
The Ending of the Posen Masters' Chess Tournament

Before the start of the last round, adjourned games were played. Kieninger showed some resistance against Keres, but was forced by his opponent into a mating net. Eysser was not able to convert his better position into a win and had to be satisfied with a draw. The decisive game for the second prize was played in the last round between Gruenfeld and Rogmann and it developed into a complex position. Gruenfeld offered a draw on his eighteenth move. Rogmann refused as the position still contained a lot of possibilities for further fight. Rogmann complicated the position, but it turned against him. He overlooked a tactical possibility in the middlegame and lost. Gruenfeld thus secured second prize. In the game between Kieninger and Bickenbach, the player from Munich won easily.

Ostdeutscher Beobachter, 1943.05.28

P.Keres *White*
Eysser *Black*
Poznan, 26 May 1943
Caro-Kann Defence

1 e4 c6 2 d4 d5 3 exd5 cxd5 4 c4 ♘f6 5 ♘c3 ♘c6 6 ♗g5 e6 7 c5 ♗e7 8 ♗b5 ♗d7 9 ♘f3 0-0 10 0-0 ♘e4 11 ♗xe7 ♘xe7 12 ♗d3 f5 13 ♘e2 ♘g6 14 b4 a6 15 a4 ♕c7 16 ♕b3 b5 17 axb5 ♗xb5 18 ♗xb5 axb5 19 ♕d3 ♕c6 20 ♘e5 ♘xe5 21 dxe5 ♖xa1 22 ♖xa1 ♖a8 23 ♖a3 ♖xa3 24 ♕xa3 d4 25 f3 ♘d2 26 ♕d3 ♘c4 27 ♕xd4 ♕a8 28 ♕d7 1-0

Paul Keres: Photographs and Games, Tallinn 1995, p158

Keres convincingly won the tournament. Gruenfeld was also successful. Rogmann, who during two and a half years has not played a single tournament game because of his 'Truppenbetreuung' chess engagements for soldiers in conquered areas, could easily have sprung a large surprise. Eysser, who for the past year and a half, has been engaged in delivering chess amusement for soldiers (and who organizing the chess 'Truppenbetreuung') has also not played any tournament games, also came very close to springing a surprise. Eysser's extensive efforts kept him from playing his best. Kieninger and Bickenbach were defeated only after stout resistance.

The press from the Varta District showed great interest in the tournament. Many radio reports were dedicated to the event. Listeners from Posen and Litzmannstadt *[Lodz—T.L.]* suggested to Secretary Majer that every Saturday at 4.30 P. M., the radio should have a Wehrmacht chess report. The first such report was aired on June 5th.

Deutsche Schachzeitung, 1943, p56

Keres' post-war chess activities are well known; it is not necessary to recount them here. Ernst Gruenfeld lived in Vienna until his death. Though not rich, he was never poor or hungry. Georg Kieninger (1902-1975) was the champion of West Germany in 1947, and during the next ten years remained one of the best chess masters in his country. But many stories are yet to be written. For example, whatever happened to Rogmann and Eysser, those tireless participants of 'Wehrmachtbetreuung'? Did Obergefreite Bickenbach survive the war? What became of those who defeated Keres in the Posen simul for the Wehrmacht: Sonderfuehrer Lau, Barthell, Jannasch, Popp, and Sonderfuehrer Waeber, who also received the award for the fastest win over the Estonian grandmaster? Will anybody ever be able to answer such questions?

Chess Archaeology (www.chessarch.com/arch.shtml)

C/ Websites

1) At Kray's: Chess Games *
www.iae.nl/users/kray/tgames.htm

Headers: *Sicilian, King's Indian*

A fairly arbitrary selection of games to download, restricted to several thousand games for the following ECO codes: B33, B78, B92, B60 and E97. Not only is the choice of openings limited, but the site is rarely updated, and for the E97 games it remains a mystery why the two zipped files are in different formats.

2) The Bristol & District Chess League *****
www.chinese-rooms.com/bristolchess

Headers: *League Information, Events, History, Games, Club Information, Results and Tables, 4NCL*

Although fixtures, club information and the results of league and cup matches can be found here, this site is far more than just your typical local league chess production. It justifies its inclusion in this chapter by offering a wealth of interesting historical articles and games to download from events in the Bristol area between 1819 and the present day.

Chris Ravilious writes about a dispute in the 1860 Bristol-Cardiff match, whilst all four volumes of John Burt's rare 1883 history of *The Bristol Chess Club* have been made available online. If Blackburne losing to the 13-year-old son of W.G. Grace in 1888 is not your cup of tea, then there is an article on the BBC's Master Game series final held in Bath in 1983 and full archives of the Website for the past four seasons, featuring many interesting tournament reports, including John Richards' articles on Bristol's performances in the 4NCL.

3) BritBase *****
www.bcmchess.co.uk/britbase
Headers: *What's New, Coming Soon, Most Wanted, Utilities, 'Korrection Korner', Pittsburgh Archive, 1920s Tournaments, 1930s Tournaments, 1940s Tournaments, 1950s Tournaments, 1960s Tournaments, 1970s Tournaments, 1980s Tournaments, 1990s Tournaments, 2000s Tournaments*

The ultimate British games and photographs archive, BritBase has been emulated across the world by such sites as Argenbase, Czechbase, Danbase, Dutchbase, Italbase, SWebase and Ukrbase. Webmaster John Saunders is scrupulously accurate, inputting thousands of games from many tournaments himself and correcting old mistakes in 'Korrection Korner', whilst he also has a 'Most Wanted' section where he asks for bulletins from certain events, so as to record those games too.

Gamescores from the most recent international events in the UK tend to appear here very soon after the event, as organisers realise how important it is to have their event recorded on Britbase, and Saunders is constantly inputting games from events in previous decades. There is now also excellent information on certain players, matches and tournaments, along with some photographs from the 1920s and 1930s.

4) Chess Archaeology *****
www.chessarch.com/arch.shtml
Headers: *Excavations, Library, Museum, Journal, Market, Openings*

Each page on this site is headed by a quote from Wilhelm Steinitz: "Chess is a scientific game and its literature ought to be placed on the basis of the strictest truthfulness, which is the foundation of all scientific research." To this end, Jacques N. Pope has set out to unearth chess secrets, which have in most cases been buried for a century or more.

Articles by amateur sleuths on topics such as 'One Man's Mind' and 'The N.Y.S.C.A's Mid-Summer Meeting at Saragota Springs 1899' are presented here ('Excavations' section) with gamescores, diagrams and photographs. Long-standing errors are corrected and new facts are brought to light. In addition, there is a bulletin board, or 'Journal', where researchers such as Ken Whyld, Richard Forster and John Donaldson ask for assistance with their projects or help to answer others' queries; a library of games from a few famous 19th-century matches; an archive of old photographs and excerpts from works by Caissa Editions ('Museum'); and a list of all the names of the opening variations under each ECO code.

5) Chess Archive ***
members.xoom.com/_XMCM/chessdata/index.htm

Headers: *Players, Openings library*

This site's claim to be the "biggest chess games library on the Web" is far from the truth, as ChessLab has two million games while Chess Archive has a mere 42,000. However, the selection here should be ample for the club player who wants to see some top class games by the likes of Kasparov, Bareev, Beliavsky, Benko, Evans, Fischer, Gelfand and many others. In total there are over 20,000 games of 23 'great grandmasters', whilst if instead, you want to look at games for a certain opening, there is no difficulty in finding all the relevant games in the archive.

For four of the five ECO code letters, 'A', 'B', 'C' and 'E', there are between 3,000 and 10,000 grandmaster games available, whilst games from openings classified under 'D' are promised soon. However, strong player and database enthusiasts will probably consider the total number of games available a little small, and they will also be strongly critical of Chess Archive's topicality, as many of the files, such as John Nunn's games, have not been updated since 1995, although for each player there are plenty of games, with Nunn having over 900.

6) ChessBase *****
www.chessbase.com

Headers: *Online Database, New Products, Events, Shop, Support, Contents*

Pricecheck: *ChessBase 7.0 Starter Package DM299.00/152.88 euros, Fritz6 DM98.00/50.11 euros, ChessBase Magazine DM195.00/99.70 euros for annual subscription (six editions on CD-Rom)*

Not exactly a database, more a support service for the database, which has become indispensable to every professional player in the world. Millions of amateur players also use ChessBase and ChessBase products such as Fritz6. The fact that this site is available in English, German and Spanish versions, shows just how popular ChessBase is. The software itself is so complex that very few people understand all of its capabilities, which is why the explanatory articles here are so useful. Steve Lopez writes a regular column about the vagaries and possibilities of ChessBase programs, answering questions on troubleshooting and giving advice to new users.

ChessBase has recently moved much more on to the Internet by providing a free online database with over 1.8 million games. This is quite similar to ChessLab, employing a Java applet board with weekly updates, although the screen layout is less cramped and the search facilities are slightly faster on ChessBase Online. The FAQs and help files for this are still a little on the small side, although they do answer most questions—for example explaining what software to download if all you see is a blank screen. As with ChessLab, the download facility is not wonderful, although we are promised that "in the next release of the ChessBase program, access to the online database will be integrated". Non-Chessbase owners should still find this a very useful resource, and they may like to explore the Playerbase to find pictures, Elo profiles, and to load the games of their favourite players or potential opponents.

Other good features of this site are the round-by-round reports on events in which ChessBase engines participate, such as Junior 6 in Dortmund, and an online shop where ChessBase products can be purchased directly, whilst there is plenty of information available on most products before you decide to buy. There are also very good demo versions including ChessBase Light, which has nearly as many functions as the main program itself.

The 'Contents' section is also worth checking out, as items not obviously available from the other pages can be found here, such as the ChessBase Magazine archive. This provides plenty of information on what was in each issue of this high-quality CD-based bimonthly magazine, which usually contains over a thousand annotated games, multimedia reports, and many other regular features by the likes of Alex Baburin and Danny King.

7) ChessLab *****
www.chesslab.com

Headers: *Two million interactive chess games online, Play Chess, Play Checkers, Chess Basics, Checkers Basics, Contact, ChessFlash News by Jude Acers, Kasparov vs. World Match Daily Commentary, FIDE World Championship —Las Vegas 1999, World Tours by Chessmaster Acers, The Greatest Chessbook of All Time, Game Basics, History, Rules, ChessLab references on the Web, ChessLab in Press, Letters from ChessLab users*

ChessLab is undoubtedly the best free database on the Web, with over two million games updated weekly. Searching is either by player or position, although player searches are usually faster, and the games found can then be either played through on the provided Java-based board or downloaded. The download feature allows up to 50 games to be downloaded from your search results at a time and the games then appear on the screen in text form, which can apparently be saved in PGN format. It is not, however, particularly easy to convert the search results into a PGN file which ChessBase can read, and so it may be worth downloading, from another site, a .pgn to .cbh converter.

ChessLab is provided by GameColony.com, who also allow you to play chess or checkers online, and chat at the same time. Other special features include chess news every couple of weeks by Jude Acers, who has also supplied several interesting articles, including a diary of the Kasparov-Rest of the World Internet match. There are several interesting book recommendations and reviews, but Acers has singled out *Logical Chess Move-by-Move* by Chernev as the greatest book ever. If European readers are wondering why they should read Acers, apparently he has made "more than 1,000 chess appearances in 48 states [and] 9 countries" since 1968, holds two simultaneous world records, and goes on chess tours in the USA.

8) ChessTutor ***
home.swipnet.se/~w-28968

Headers: *Online Chess Openings Library, Sample Games, Download ChessTutor, Comments and suggestions*

Here you can find all about using ChessTutor on a Website, in particular, that it allows anyone with a Java-enabled Web browser to play through games online, without needing any specialist programs, such as ChessBase. With ChessTutor, it is possible to create and collect PGN files and then play through all the games. For a good example of ChessTutor in action visit the Website of the Smith & Williamson Young Masters (*www.swyoungmasters.co.uk*).

9) G. Ossimitz: Chess-Page *****
www.crosswinds.net/~ossimitz/chess.htm

Headers: *guestbook, player, event, from books, tactic, curious, bookstore, mail, Annofritzed Game Collections of Famous Players, Recent Tournaments and Matches—annofritzed!, Classical Tournaments and Matches—annofritzed!, Games Collections from Books, Tactical Test Positions, Collections of Chess Curiosities, My Chess Book Store, My favorite chess books!, Chess-book bestsellers at Amazon!, How to read/analyze CBH-formatted files, Annofritzation Time Settings, Copyright issues, Please Contribute!, Partner Sites*

Yet another vast database of downloadable games? Not quite. The advantage of Ossimitz's games is that he or a contributor has 'Annofritzed' them—i.e. they have set the Fritz5 analysis engine running to produce annotations. This might sound like a simple task, but it is time-consuming, so the computer program has usually been given five seconds per move, a long way from its deepest analysis. In the file of

Bobby Fischer's 'My 60 Memorable Games', however, you can compare Fritz's five-second setting with its annotations after 90 seconds per move. As Ossimitz points out, Fritz is not infallible. "Please, take the Fritz-annotations just for fun," he says. "They give sometimes useful hints about possible variations or improvements, sometimes they are just nonsense." There is rarely anything wrong with the games themselves, which are mostly taken from classic chess books, whilst there are several tactical positions for use as self-tests.

The 'Curiosities' section provides zipped files of games on a wide range of different topics. These include about 1,400 games featuring a ...♖xc3 sacrifice; games featuring underpromotions; a collection of over 20 different GM and computer annotations of the superb classic Kasparov-Topalov, Wijk aan Zee 1999; a report with games on the Myanmar ratings scandal; and an excellent annofritzed collection of over 75,000 GM games.

10) The Irish Chess Archive *****
www.markorr.net/tica

Headers: *What's New, Index, Game Index, Gallery, Players' Profiles, Championships, Team Tournaments, FIDE Ratings, Tournaments, Quizzes, Acknowledgements, TICA in the Press, Help*

An enthralling guide to Irish chess players and their games. So you've never heard of any Irish players, huh? How about Alexander McDonnell, famous for his match with Louis Charles de la Bourdonnais; James Mason, whose real name was revealed by a brilliant piece of detective work; Brian Reilly, who beat Reuben Fine in 1935 and became editor of *British Chess Magazine*; Eamon Keogh, who beat Gideon Stahlberg and is Ireland's biggest raconteur; and Russian GM Alexander Baburin, now resident in Dublin and captain of the Irish Olympiad team in 1996. Even people with no connection to Irish chess will soon want to know more after visiting this site, not least to score a few points in the trivia quizzes.

Webmaster Mark Orr gathers his source material from all over the place—if an Irish player has ever been interviewed, that interview will probably appear on TICA. Vincent Maher, who was born in 1929 and won the Irish Championship twice, contributed his own brief autobiography. In it we learn that Maher's chess teacher joined the RUC and was shot dead, and that Maher himself was a captain in the British Army Medical Corps, attending Rudolf Hess and Albert Speer in Spandau jail.

David McAlister performs much sterling research for TICA, including—assisted by Swiss IM Richard Forster—a superb biography of the first Irish Champion, Porterfield Rynd. Hundreds of games can be downloaded from this thorough site, which also contains results from all the Irish

Championships since 1865, Irish international congresses, such as Kilkenny and Bunratty, and Ireland's performances in the Olympiads and European Team Championships. Orr presents excellent coverage of the Elista Olympiad, whilst his coverage and diary from Batumi, where he played on top board for Ireland, is also enjoyable and well worth reading. He can certainly use most aspects of modern technology very well. For instance, there are many good pictures taken by digital camera on the site, whilst Orr is surely one of the first Webmasters to make his site accessible to WAP-enabled mobile phones.

11) La Mecca Chess Encyclopaedia *****
maskeret.com/mecca/index.shtml

Headers: *Who, When and Where, Companion, About this site, Other sites of mine*

This links database by Italian player and tournaments director, Maurizio Mascheroni (nickname 'maskeret'), can be searched alphabetically or by keyword, so that all the relevant chess resources on the Web appear instantly at your fingertips. If you look up 'Steinitz', for instance, you will be pointed to '1876: Match between Messrs Blackburne and Steinitz' by Jacques Pope, '1894: Lasker-Steinitz World Championship' by Jack Pope and 'A big step forward' by Ignacio Marin. If you search 'the complete index' by letter, say 'T', you will get a long list which begins, 'Tactics; Taimanov, Mark (1926-); Taiwan; Tajikistan; Tal, Mikhail Nekhemievich (1936-1992); Tallinn; Tamborino, Pasquale; Tamerlane (1336-1405); Tarjan, James (1952-); Tarrasch Variation.' This gives a hint of the enormous scope of 'maskeret's' undertaking.

'Who, When and Where' presents information about over 3,000 players, together with images of most of them, whilst there is also information on over 1,000 tournaments. A timeline may well interest chess historians, who can also see what happened 'today in the history'. There is also an option to convert your national rating to Elo or to find out someone else's FIDE rating, whilst a database of chess-related press releases called 'BLIP' can be searched by keyword. The 'Roulette' feature is an interesting idea and brings up ten sites randomly for you to explore, and frequent visitors to this gateway to chess on the Internet will find all the new links on 'The What's New Page', which is updated each week.

12) La Régence ***
www.notzai.com/notzai/regence/regence.shtml

Headers: *None (games are categorised by opening)*

This section of Pascal 'Notzai' Villalba's French site is also available in English, and La Régence contains hundreds of thousands of games from 1997 onwards. These games are culled from other Internet databases including TWIC, Pittsburgh University, Britbase and Danbase. You can download files which relate to a particular opening, but you can't search by player or event, whilst the site can go for more than four months without being updated.

13) Lars Balzer's Homepage *****
www.rhrk.uni-kl.de/~balzer/index.html
Headers: *Chessgames Links, Chess Download, Guestbook*

If you want to collect hundreds of thousands of games for free then a visit to German, Lars Balzer's page, is essential. The only games for download directly from the site are those for the 1995-9 German Junior Championships, but then the site is mainly about links to other sites where games can be downloaded for free.

Balzer has more links to game archive sites than anywhere else on the Web, and the hundred or so of them are listed by country. Germany, probably due to Balzer's nationality, has the most, but even countries which one would not really associate with chess, such as Trinidad and Tobago and Uruguay, have games collections which can be accessed direct from Balzer's links. To ensure that you don't miss any new additions to any of the archive sites, Balzer even mentions when they were last updated. There is also an e-mail newsletter which explains when his site, and thus the sites with links on his site, have been updated.

14) Observer's Games from chess.net *
www.homestead.com/observer/PGNs.html
Headers: *Go to the Players request page, Go to The Titled Player page, Go to the Encyclopedia of Chess Openings page*

Terry Bohannon offers to search for games for members of chess.net and will find games either by player or opening and post the results in PGN format on this site. Whether the ten games collections on the site, which refused to download, and were unzipped and several megabytes in size anyway, are old requests is not clear, but if they are then this service is rarely used. This may well be because members of chess.net would be put off by the awful layout on all the main pages of this site; text frequently overlaps or covers up labelled hyperlinks. If you can stand this then you will find games to download by, along with a brief biography and a photo of, ten grandmasters (Karpov, Judit Polgar, Bacrot, Dzindzichashvili, Shirov, Alekhine, Kasparov, Spassky, Botvinnik and Petrosian).

The openings page gives names to the lines under each ECO code, whilst between several hundred to several thousand games from each code, can be downloaded in PGN format. Should you really want to, it is possible to see statistics for each code. For example, "A00 has 1749536 moves from 25123 games. There are 1433677 unique positions. Maximum ply count is 310 plies", but this is not really useful information, and sometimes more and other times less than the number of games used in the statistics can be downloaded.

15) Pitt Chess Archives *****
www3.pitt.edu/~schach/Archives/index2.html
Headers: *Newstuff, Games Collections, Chess Materials*

A seemingly bottomless pit (excuse the pun) of chess material, with thousands of games available for download, in Chess Assistant, ChessBase, PGN, NicBase and Bookup formats, on every conceivable opening. The newsgroup *rec.games.chess.misc* will update you about any additions. There is also some gimmicky stuff, such as photos of famous players which can be downloaded—to become pin-ups in your bedroom, perhaps, and some useful stuff, including database format conversion programs available for download.

The main weaknesses of this site are its unfriendliness, bland layout, and fact that only 50 users are allowed to be on the pages, held at Pittsburgh University, at one time. It is also fairly easy to become lost amongst reams of filenames like adamsjpg.zip, deadpn1.zip and immortal.zip; therefore you should load a file called 'allindex.txt', which, assuming that you are using a browser with a find feature, can be searched for the filename of the tournament, opening, or whatever else you wish to download.

16) Rob Weir's ChessBase Utilities ****
www.cybercom.net/~rweir/cbutil.htm
Headers: *None*

For those out there still using Chessbase versions 1.0-5.0 (i.e. pre-.cbh format users), and experiencing problems with them, then you can find a number of free little programs for download here, to make managing, searching and using your databases a lot easier. It is possible to appreciate and use Weir's creations without any programming knowledge. These perform tasks, such as to "normalize game spelling, punctuation, user-defined substitutions, etc.", or to generate "performance statistics based on ECO code". The FAQs are fairly useful, although those without any technical knowledge will struggle to understand them, and they may explain why this site has not been updated since 1998, because when .cbh format was launched with ChessBase 6.0, "the publishers of ChessBase [chose] not to document the new file format", without which Weir cannot create any more helpful little programs!

17) "Schaak!" ***
www.gironet.nl/home/kooij97/index.htm
Headers: *games, sites, more information, guestbook*

The defunct *"Schaak!"* publication's editor, Jaap van der Kooij from the Netherlands, offers a selection of games by a different strong player every fortnight, such as CC GM Jonathan Penrose. *"Schaak!"* is a "former well-known booklet with over 100 corr. games" and was moved onto the Web in May 1997. It is no longer produced in print form. Van der Kooij has a massive personal database of 2,835,278 games, and he offers games from a new back issue of *"Schaak!"* every fortnight, with three issues available online at one time. These usually contain a few thousand games for download, in either zipped ChessBase or zipped NicBase formats, all on the same opening line, such as the Classical Pirc or the Cunningham variation of the King's Gambit.

To enable newcomers to eventually have all the games from *"Schaak!"*, van der Kooij has restarted with *"Schaak!"* 001, so there are two cycles of back issues in progress. Many of the games in the back issues are not available in BigBase 2000, and so are worth having; unlike the 'Theory' section games, which are a waste of time to download, consisting of unannotated games, just a few opening moves in length.

18) Uncrowned Kings *****
www.phileo.demon.co.uk
Headers: *File*

Originally established to collect games for download in zipped ChessBase format by, and photographs of, players who, "were not granted the opportunity, for various reasons, to play a match for the world title". Uncrowned Kings now also includes files on the Hypermoderns (Gyula Breyer, Ernst Gruenfeld, Richard Réti and Saviely Tartakower), and on British Champions (so far Howard Staunton, Frederick Yates, Sir George Thomas and Mir Sultan Khan). The Uncrowned Kings themselves are Paul Keres, Aron Nimzowitsch, Akiba Rubinstein, Bent Larsen and Victor Korchnoi.

Webmaster Phil Hughes hopes to eventually offer every game played by all these people, and he believes that the Keres file may already be complete with 2,011 games. The site is regularly updated, and an index shows clearly what was updated and when; whilst for certain players Hughes has a target number of games, and even lists the missing Nimzowitsch games, inviting contributions for these.

7
Analysis

Many chess Websites contain some annotated games, but far fewer concentrate on analysis. It is a treat to read each issue of GM Alexander Baburin's newsletter, *Coffee Break Chess*, while the other sites featured here are immensely enjoyable and of a high standard.

A/ Webmaster Hall of Fame

Chris White, ChessPublishing

Please introduce yourself

Chris White, founder of ChessPublishing.com. My background is TV and video, although I have also been running a chess business since I set up Grandmaster Video in the late 1980s.

Where did the idea of ChessPublishing come from?

The original idea for ChessPublishing evolved over a few beers with Nigel Davies while (or I guess after) we were recording one of the videos for the Foxy Openings series. The ever-increasing number of games published every week on the Internet is no joke. These days many books are out of date before they are even published, and even most GMs and professionals will admit they can't keep up. The blueprint for

ChessPublishing was to put together a team of grandmasters and leading authors who would trawl through this cybermountain of new games to dig out the gems and nuggets—then offer in-depth coverage of the secrets and stories behind any important opening developments.

Basically ChessPublishing tries to make some sense out of the ongoing opening fashion show hosted on the Internet, providing peace of mind to those who want to keep track of their favourite lines, or sparks of inspiration to those who want something new. The emphasis is on high-quality insight and explanation.

Do you think that Internet chess clubs will gradually supplant real chess clubs? Do you play chess on the Internet—if so, where?

I play a bit of blitz on the ICC, but almost always while I'm on the phone or watching TV. Personally I also like coffee bar chess. I suppose that's just because I'm generally happier when there's plenty of conversation or background noise. I know that real chess clubs are struggling to attract new members but I don't think they can blame the Internet for that.

How easy was it to create the Website and choose your openings experts?

It was really a matter of finding the right coding experts and a good designer who could handle such an ambitious site (I don't have any IT skills myself). ChessPublishing also has a sophisticated content management and database subscription system, as well as its own secure online multicurrency payment system. The site generates automatic royalty statements for the authors, who get paid on the basis of subscriptions and clicks/revenue to their zones. It is a transparent publishing framework in which authors can continually monitor the popularity of their own pages.

I was keen to go for top authors who seem to enjoy writing with plenty of punch and verve, who would be at home in the more informal surrounds of the Internet. I made up a shortlist of GMs who I wanted to invite to write for ChessPublishing, and luckily it was not too difficult to persuade them. The 12 big-name writers are undoubtedly one of the main attractions behind ChessPublishing.

How popular is the site and do you receive positive feedback from subscribers?

It's not unusual to get a couple of million hits per month, but of course it's been very rewarding to attract large numbers of subscribers from the outset. The power of the Internet means that we have subscribers in almost every country you can imagine, but not surprisingly, the majority of our subscribers come from the US.

We do receive a lot of feedback and yes it is invariably positive. Subscribers love to e-mail the experts with queries about their own pet lines, and often wonder what to do about stuff that they have to face down at their local club, but which doesn't get a mention in any of the books. If we get several requests along the same lines then we will often commission new features for the site, such as the 'Repertoire Recommendations'.

How happy have you been with the amount of effort by your openings experts?

Very happy and I really mean it! Before we even launched online, each of the guys prepared over 150 pages of original content for their section, which is more material than in many books! There's no doubt that the site offers excellent value for money—it's pretty staggering to think that we have already published over 5,000 pages in our first year, since we launched in September 1999.

What are your future plans for the site?

We have all sorts of new developments in the pipeline. With the commercial future of the site assured, we are now in a position to design the next generation blueprint for ChessPublishing.com. I can't go into details, but some of the most interesting new ideas have been suggested by subscribers—if there is something you would particularly like to see at ChessPublishing.com then please send an e-mail to *newideas@chesspublishing.com*.

B/ Best of the Web
Coffee Break Chess' No. 15, 11th September 1999

© 1999 by Alexander Baburin

Dear Chess Friends!

After two tournaments in England, I am back to Dublin and finally I have an opportunity to produce a proper issue of CBC. My readership is growing fast and I hope that you will enjoy this issue. Here I am going to look at recent events and show one of my games.

Alexander Khalifman is the new FIDE World Champion. The championship in Las Vegas saw some surprises, as Elo-favourites were knocked out at various stages and the tournament produced an unexpected winner. Still, Khalifman has always been highly respected among chess professionals as a player of high class and big potential, who possibly did not get too many chances to show his true abilities. In Vegas he played good chess and showed a lot of psychological stubbornness, which is crucial in tournaments with a knock-out format. Khalifman's victory is well received among his colleagues.

After the championship, Alexander gave a very balanced interview to a Russian newspaper, which I saw on the Net. There he said that Kasparov is the strongest player in the world at present, but the tournament in Vegas was the only real world championship. He said that in Vegas, high rating did not guarantee victory, even to such strong players as Kramnik and Shirov, which is only normal in any sport—otherwise prizes would be distributed according to ratings. Khalifman says that he is as devoted to his 'Grandmaster Chess School' as ever and he will continue to develop it. You can find it at http://www.gmchess.spb.ru/ index.html. There is also an interview with Khalifman in English—at *http://www1.worldfide.com/chess/press36.html.*

Many sites covered the Vegas championship and Kasparov followed it on his Web page—*http://www.clubkasparov.ru/ index0e.htm.*

Alas, he seems to find dubious joy in insulting other players. A few years ago Kasparov coined the term, "real chess player", making most players "unreal". While recently he came out with the name, "tourists". I guess that such an attitude only damages his image.

From what I heard from those who played in Vegas, it's clear that GMs just want to have some system in the chess world, where they can show their professional abilities and also play for decent prizes. FIDE had lots of problems organizing the championship in Vegas, but at least did manage it—let's hope that FIDE will get more efficient in the future. Meanwhile there is no news about the Kasparov-Anand match (at least, I have not seen any).

Mind Sports Olympiad

Between 21st-29th of August, I played in this rather strong tournament (18 GMs) in London. There I played better than in the recent British Championship. Going into the final round, I was a point ahead of my rivals. Alas, in round 9 I lost to Jon Speelman and thus failed to win the event outright. The results were as follows: 1-3. A.Baburin (IRL) (gold medal), I.Psakhis (ISR) (silver) and J.Speelman (ENG) (bronze)—7 points out of 9. 4-7. M.Chandler (ENG), Y.Murey (ISR), I.Smirin (ISR), Y.Zilberman (ISR) 6½ out of 9.

I wrote about this tournament at http://www.chesscafe.com/ world/report/england.htm.

There I annotated my game against GM Ibragimov and some other games from the event. My new book review is also out at 'Chess Cafe'—*http://www.chesscafe.com/baburin/ baburin. htm.*

You can chat with me online. I'll participate in a live chat at *http://chess.about.com/mpchat.htm*, conducted by David Dunbar, on Sunday the 26th of September at 16:00 Eastern US time. This is 21:00 London time, or 22:00 Central European time. Everyone is welcome to the chat, so please take a note and let's meet there. You can familiarise yourself with the way such chats work by checking previous sessions: *http://chess.about.com/library/weekly/aa050399.htm* (chat with GM Rohde) and *http://chess.about.com/library/weekly/aa053199.htm* (chat with IM Silman). Prepare your questions and suggestions and let's discuss them!

Annotated game

Here I would like to show one of my games from London, which saw a very fashionable opening line, an interesting middlegame, and a very curious rook ending.

V. Mikhalevski (2516) *White*
A. Baburin *Black*
Mind Sports Olympiad, Round 8
August 28, 1999

1 d4 d5 2 c4 dxc4 3 ♘f3 a6 4 e3 e6 5 ♗xc4 c5 6 0-0 ♘f6 7 ♗b3 cxd4 8 exd4 ♘c6 9 ♘c3 ♗e7 10 ♖e1 0-0 11 a3 b5
Black often plays 11...♘a5 12 ♗c2 b5, but then White can sacrifice a pawn with 13 d5!?.
12 d5 exd5 13 ♘xd5 ♘xd5 14 ♗xd5
After 14 ♕xd5 in the game against GM Morovic in Havana this year, I showed a very important novelty: 14...♘a5! (14...♗b7 15 ♕h5 leaves White with initiative). Ivan did not dare to take on a8 and after 15 ♕xd8 ♗xd8 16 ♗d5 ♗b7 17 ♗xb7 ♘xb7 18 ♗f4 ♗f6 19 ♗e5 ♗xe5 20 ♘xe5 the game was soon drawn.
14...♗b7 15 ♘e5
After 15 ♗f4 ♗f6 16 ♖c1 ♖c8 17 b4 ♕d7 18 ♘g5 ♗xg5 19 ♗xg5 ♖fe8 20 ♖xe8+ ♖xe8 21 ♗f3 ♕xd1+ 22 ♖xd1 ♗a8 23 ♗f4 ♘e7 24 ♗xa8 ♖xa8 25 ♖d7 ♘g6 Black equalised in the game Schandorff-Baburin (Copenhagen, 1999), which later ended in a draw.
15...♘xe5 16 ♗xb7 ♖a7 17 ♗e4 ♗f6 18 ♗e3
White also did not get any edge in the game Avrukh-Har Zvi (Tel Aviv, 1999), after 18 ♕b3 ♖d7 19 ♕h3 g6 20 ♗h6 ♗g7 21 ♗xg7 ♔xg7.
18...♖d7 19 ♕c2 g6 20 ♖ad1 ♘c4 21 ♗c1
White has nothing after 21 ♗c5 ♖e8 22 ♖xd7 (22 ♗c6? ♖xe1+ 23 ♖xe1 ♖d2 24 ♕e4 ♗xb2 is bad for White.) 22...♕xd7 23 b3 ♘d2.
21...♖e8 22 ♗f3?

White fails to see that his back rank is weak... Better was 22 ♗c6 ♖xe1+ 23 ♖xe1 ♖e7 24 ♖xe7 ♕xe7 25 g3=.

22...♗xb2!

Also possible is 22...♖xe1+ 23 ♖xe1 ♗xb2 24 ♗xb2 ♖d2.

23 ♗xb2 ♘xb2 24 ♖xe8+ ♕xe8 25 ♖f1 ♘d3 26 ♕c6 ♕e6!

I did not see anything decisive after 26...♘e5 27 ♕xa6 ♘xf3+ 28 gxf3 ♖d5 29 ♖c1.

27 ♕c8+ ♔g7 28 ♗b7 ♘c5

Here White had only two minutes left, but unfortunately I failed to make life harder for him. I saw the line 28...♘xf2! 29 ♕c3+ f6 30 ♕c6, but did not see that after 30...♕xc6 31 ♗xc6 ♖d6 32 ♗xb5 I could play 32...♘h3+!, which should be winning for me after 33 gxh3 axb5 34 ♖b1 ♖d5 35 ♖b4 f5 36 a4 bxa4 37 ♖xa4 ♔f6 38 ♖a7 h6.

29 ♕xc5 ♖xb7 30 ♖c1 ♖e7 31 h4 ♕e5 32 ♕b4 h5 33 g3 ♖e6 34 ♖c8 ♕e1+ 35 ♔g2 ♕e4+ 36 ♔g1 ♕xb4 37 axb4 ♔f6

I doubt that Black can win after 37...♖e4 38 ♖c6 ♖xb4 39 ♖xa6 ♖b2 40 ♖b6 b4 41 ♔g2 b3 42 ♔f3 ♔f8 43 ♖b7. I think I was right to leave the b4-pawn. Though at present this pawn stops two of my pawns, later it can turn into a weakness itself.

38 ♖c5 ♖b6 39 ♔f1 ♔e6 40 ♔e2 ♔d6 41 ♖c8 ♖c6 42 ♖f8 ♔e7 43 ♖a8 ♔e6 44 ♖a7

44...♔d5!

I think this move is better than 44...♖c4 45 ♖xa6+ ♔f5 46 ♖a7 f6 47 ♖b7 ♖xb4 48 ♖b6 ♖b3. Now after 45 ♖xf7 ♔c4 46 ♖f4+ ♔b3 Black threatens to sacrifice yet another pawn by ...a5 and to get his b-pawn rolling, while White can't play 47 g4, because of 47...♖c4! 48 ♖f6 ♖xg4 49 ♖xa6 ♔xb4. Thus, White preferred to stop the advance of Black's king:

45 ♔d3 ♖f6! 46 f4 ♖d6 47 ♖c7 f5

I believe that Black benefits from fixing pawns on the kingside. He could not utilise the f5-square anyway. Now even if Black sacrifices the g6-pawn, it will be very hard for White to create a passed pawn there. It's important that Black's rook defends both weak pawns on the same horizontal, leaving the king with some freedom to manoeuvre.

48 ♖c8 ♔e6+ 49 ♔c3 ♔d7 50 ♖g8 ♔c6 51 ♖c8+ ♔b6 52 ♖b8+ ♔a7 53 ♖c8 ♔b7 54 ♖g8 ♔c7 55 ♖a8 ♖c6+ 56 ♔d4

After 56 ♔b3 I would play 56...♔d6 57 ♖d8+ ♔e6, threatening to penetrate with the king along the d-file. For example: 58 ♖d1 ♖d6 59 ♖e1+ ♔d5 60 ♖d1+ ♔c6 61 ♖c1+ ♔b6 62 ♖c3 a5 or 58 ♔b2 ♖d6 59 ♖e8+ ♔d5 60 ♔c3 ♖e6 61 ♖d8+ ♔e4.

56...♔b7 57 ♖g8

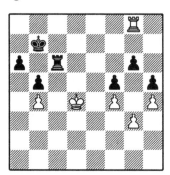

75...a5!

It was hard to choose between this move and the line 57...♖c4+!? 58 ♔d5 ♖xb4 59 ♖g7+ (59 ♖xg6 ♖b3 60 ♖g5 a5 61 ♖xf5 a4 62 ♖xh5 a3 63 ♖h7+ ♔b6 64 ♖h6+ ♔a5 65 ♖h8 ♔b4 66 ♖a8 ♖xg3 is even worse) 59...♔b6 60 ♖xg6+ ♔a5. After 61 ♖g5 ♖b3 62 ♖xh5 ♖xg3 63 ♖xf5 ♔b4 black pawns are more dangerous than their counterparts, but 57...a5! looked even more attractive to me.

58 bxa5 b4 59 ♔d5?

Here White missed the last chance to put up more resistance with 59 ♖e8! ♔a6 60 ♔d5 ♖c3 61 ♖e6+ ♔xa5 62 ♖xg6 b3.

59...b3 60 ♖g7+ ♖c7 61 ♖xg6 ♔a7!

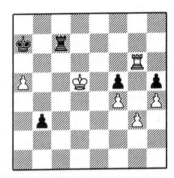

This is what White missed—now he can't stop the b-pawn. Moving the king to the corner does not look very aesthetic, but now Black's rook can support the b-pawn from behind, e.g., White immediately loses after 62 ♖b6 ♖b7 63 ♔c4 b2.

62 ♔e5 ♖c5+ 63 ♔d4 ♖b5 64 ♔c4

White is also doomed after 64 ♖b6 ♖xb6 65 axb6+ ♔xb6 66 ♔c3 ♔c5 67 ♔xb3 ♔d4 68 ♔b4 ♔e3 69 ♔c5 ♔f3 70 ♔d5 ♔xg3 71 ♔e5 ♔g4.

64...♖b8 65 ♖g7+ ♔a6 66 ♖g6+ ♔xa5 67 ♖d6 b2 68 ♖d5+ ♔a6 69 ♖d6+ ♖b6 0-1

(Time: 2.57—2.49)

In my previous issue, I showed two rook endgames and promised to cover them later. I will come back to them in the next issue of 'Coffee Break Chess'. Meanwhile I would like to hear your suggestions on how to make this newsletter better. Please share with me your ideas and suggestions! I am currently working on my Web page, so I hope to implement some of your suggestions there as well.

Have a nice weekend!

Alexander Baburin, *Dublin*
Alex Baburin's Web Site (ababurin.tripod.com)

C/ Websites

1) Achim's Chess Page *****
it.e-technik.uni-ulm.de/~engelhar/chess/chesspage.html
Headers: *Analysis, Combinations corner, Information, News*

Instantly and refreshingly, we are greeted by pure hypertext. Achim's Chess Page consists mainly of interesting and richly annotated games. The only graphics you'll find on the site are the chessboards. It's mainly written by Achim, but he also encourages e-mailed contributions. What's more, people actually do e-mail him, from the obviously strong Kastanas, to the even more obviously strong GM Khalifman (FIDE World Champion). It seems anyone is free to add their pennyworth. The Internet at its best.

2) Alex Baburin's Web Site ****
ababurin.tripod.com

Headers: *Chat Room, Book Shop, Profile, Endings, My Calendar, GM Forum, Chess Auctions, My Best Games, News, Chess Wonders, Puzzle Page, Game Viewer, Photo Gallery, Q and Answers, Collectors Corner, CBC Central, Alex's Book, Coaching*

Pricecheck: Moscow 1935 *43.65 euros + 35 Club Points,* 33rd Chess Olympiad, Elista 1998 *84.00 euros + 60 Club Points,* Genius in Chess *19.95 euros + 10 Club Points [Once 150 Club Points have been collected you can start using them for future purchases, with 10 Club Points equal to 1 euro.]*

This is a real potpourri of a site, including some high quality analysis. All past issues of Dublin-based Russian GM Alex Baburin's e-mail newsletter *Coffee Break Chess,* are available for download, whilst Baburin also presents endings, puzzles, and his favourite personal games. *Coffee Break Chess* started in early 1999 and after 25 issues, *CBC* has over 1,400 readers, is available in seven languages and continues to go from strength to strength. Each issue features one or two well-annotated games with diagrams, and in the midst of his annotations, Baburin often asks questions about the position which can be pondered over a cup of coffee. Moreover, *CBC* keeps readers up-to-date with Baburin's own chess activities and provides snippets of news.

Baburin's coaching services are also fully advertised on the site (one hour over the phone or Internet costs $50, whilst he will also analyse five games for $90) and, judging from his excellent annotations elsewhere, Baburin should be a great coach. His sample analysis of five games shows that he is very good at drawing students' attention to general principles, whilst he quickly picks out the areas of their game needing most attention.

The site reveals that Baburin is also a bookseller, dealing mainly in Russian works, which he supplies to such exalted customers as the Royal Dutch Library in The Hague, and an auctioneer. 'Collectors' Corner' enables chess historians to seek answers to help with their research, whilst Baburin himself provides some enlightening answers about the life of a chess professional on the 'Questions and Answers' page. Chess politics is another of Baburin's interests and readers can vote on topical items, such as drug testing, whilst also being able to read, in the GM Forum, grandmasters' views on the current state of the chess world. This site is well worth a visit, and one only hopes that Baburin will be able to keep it all updated. One piece of advice for surfers: give the usually empty chat room a miss unless Baburin is doing an online live interview.

3) ChessPublishing *****
www.chesspublishing.com

Headers: *1 e4 e5, French, Dragons, Open Sicilians, Anti-Sicilians, 1 e4 ..., 1 d4 d5, d-pawn Specials, King's Indian, Nimzo & Benoni, Daring Defences, Flank Openings, Double Trouble, Subscribe, Upgrade, Site Info, Schedule, Repertoire, GM Surfers, Free Preview, E-mail Bulletin*

Pricecheck: *1 site £14.00/22.50 euros/US$18.00 p.a., any 3 sites £28.00/45.00 euros/$36.00 p.a., Gold Card (all 12 sites) £70.00/112.50 euros/US$90.00* p.a.

ChessPublishing is possibly the future of chess, as here subscribers receive the latest annotated games in each opening, which can be either viewed online with a pop-up Java board, or downloaded into ChessBase. The writers are all respected experts on their opening (1 e4 e5—GM Paul Motwani, The French—GM Neil McDonald, Sicilian Dragons—GM Chris Ward, Open Sicilians—GM John Fedorowicz, Anti-Sicilians—IM Gary Lane, 1 e4...—GM Alexander Volzhin, 1 d4 d5 GM Ruslan Scherbakov, d-pawn Specials—GM Aaron Summerscale, Global King's Indian—IM Andrew Martin, Nimzo & Benoni Systems—GMs Chris Ward and John Emms, Daring Defences—GMs Jon Tisdall and Neil McDonald, English and other Flank Openings—GM Tony Kosten). Besides annotating all the top new games each month, they often include some 'classics' to help improve subscribers' understanding of the opening.

The annotations are generally good, although those with large topics, such as Fedorowicz, have had to mainly concentrate on games involving strong GMs and just provide a few comments to many of the other games. Special bonuses include recommended repertoires for different types of player by IM Andrew Martin and GM Nigel Davies, whilst for gold card subscribers, Paul Motwani, possibly the best of the writers, presents 'Double Trouble', which contains a number of dangerous and interesting opening ideas.

Subscribers are kept posted with the latest updates, although these tend to arrive at the end of a month, whilst feedback is always welcomed. Some sites do provide special bonuses such as quizzes, to test what subscribers have learnt. Overall, ChessPublishing is best viewed with Internet Explorer 4.0 or 5.0 and not Netscape, if you want all the gimmicks and the Java boards to work fully. It is possible to see enough material on the free preview to decide whether to subscribe, but for all serious club players, especially ChessBase users, this site with the vast amount of very recent annotated information, is highly recommended and excellent value.

4) Diemer-Duhm Gambit ****
www.funet.fi/pub/doc/games/chess/ddg

Headers: *Games, Analysis, Articles, News, Tournaments, References*

Jyrki Heikkinen from Finland, the world's leading expert on the Diemer-Duhm Gambit (1 e4 e6 2 d4 d5 3 c4, or 1 d4 d5 2 c4 e6 3 e4), has an amazing 81 per cent score with his favourite opening, including a draw against GM Bogdan Lalic. He wishes that there were a book solely on the DDG, and even provides a humorous list of potential titles, but this Website practically constitutes an entire book on the subject. The twice-yearly 'Diemer-Duhm Gambit News' provides new analyses and games, both from readers and e-mail tournaments devoted exclusively to the DDG, as well as listings of newly published articles on the DDG.

All manner of variations in the DDG are analysed in this easy to navigate site. Not only Heikkinen, but also contributors such as IM John Watson have added to the reams of analysis on the many subvariations of the DDG. Heikkinen also clearly explains the main ideas behind the opening, whilst there are hundreds of games to download for study. His enthusiasm is evident throughout, and it is hard not to be convinced that the DDG is a fun and psychologically good choice of opening.

5) GambitSite ****
thomasstock.com/gambit

Headers: *News, Download, General ChessPage, Who I am, TGT, Gambits in the Web, My Publications, SubWebs, Forum, Recommended, Discussions, Reviews, Experts, ChessBase, WebTools, Enigma*

Thomas Stock MD, from Germany, is a gambit fanatic and quite a character, who also enjoys swimming and "snorcheling" (especially in the Maldives), and stamp-collecting. His Web pages are accompanied by vigorous piano playing and can be explored in English, German, or Italian. Readers can submit their own games or analysis, and even set up their own gambit page as a 'subweb'.

Stock plays in and organises many e-mail gambit tournaments, and the games from these, along with many from other gambiteers, are available for download. His own favourite appears to be the Muzio Gambit (1 e4 e5 2 f4 exf4 3 ♘f3 g5 4 ♗c4 g4 5 0-0), about which he is writing a book on the Internet, called *The Enigma of Signor Muzio*. This features many historical publications on the Muzio, along with a wealth of detailed analysis. Stock should be taken seriously as an analyst—his work has been published in *ChessBase*

Magazine and *Informator.* Monthly News rounds up all the latest contributions to the many gambits on this site, whilst there are also extensive links to every Internet resource on gambits, and many non-Internet resources.

D/ Newsgroups

rec.games.chess.analysis **

For those looking for some grandmaster analysis, do not subscribe to this newsgroup. Approximately 50 messages are posted each week, but these are often concerned with advertising tournaments and Websites, or deal with computers. Even when discussion is on chess analysis, it is often club players desperately wanting to know what to do against a certain opening, or why a move was not played in a well-known game. That said, others do often reply and indeed there are some worthwhile postings by Eric Schiller and others, but many who subscribe are probably very weak, with one asking why 1 d4 d5 2 c4 e6 3 ♘c3 ♘f6 4 ♗g5 ♘bd7 5 cxd5 does not win a pawn (5 cxd5 exd5 6 ♘xd5?? ♘xd5! 7 ♗xd8 ♗b4+ and Black will emerge a piece ahead).

E/ Mailing Lists

1) Chess Analysis *****
chess_analysis-subscribe@onelist.com

If you are under 1800 in grade (about 150 BCF), then this is a good group to join to improve your game. Then, if you are brave, you can submit any of your games for analysis by the planet. But be warned, people really do take the trouble to look at, and comment in detail on, the games that are submitted! On the other hand, most of the submissions are polite and carry extensive analysis.

2) EnglundGambit *****
englundgambit-subscribe@egroups.com

This is what e-mail chess groups are all about, deadly gambiteers secretly sharing trade secrets. Most 1 d4 players favour a strategic game and if you're not careful you'll be fast asleep by move 5. Why not hit them with 1...e5!??, initiating immediate tactical complications? This is a small but exclusive group devoted to the Englund Gambit, which may not be as sound as the Semi-Slav, but there's a minefield of tactical tricks for our boring d4 players to defuse before they can consider that they have an edge. Many will fail and you can proudly report back to base with the news.

8
Products
& Services

Few people live within easy reach of a chess shop, but anyone with Internet access and a credit card can order books and equipment online. These online shops often offer reviews, articles and downloads to enjoy, and some of them are connected to a print magazine. Surfers can easily compare prices between online shops. Coaching services can also be found in this chapter.

A/ Webmaster Hall of Fame

John Saunders, BCM, BCF, Britbase

Please introduce yourself

I am John Saunders, 47, married, editor and co-owner of *British Chess Magazine*, editor-in-chief of *ChessMoves* (the British Chess Federation's bimonthly newsletter) and editor of the BBC Ceefax chess pages. All three of these jobs are very much hands-on, involving writing, interviewing, reviewing, analysing, editing, typesetting, Webmastering, taking photographs, buying and selling, hiring and firing, IT technical support, negotiating, administration, book-keeping... the workload can be absolutely staggering at times.

How often do you have a chance to play chess?

I refer you to the previous answer. Ironically, I have far less time to play chess, now that I work full-time in the chess world, than I ever did when working outside chess. I play in the 4NCL [Four Nations Chess League in the UK] and occasionally in a low-category international all-play-all, when the organiser needs a cheap 'foreigner' (I'm Welsh-registered).

When and why did you decide to set up a Website?

I started my original Web site—for Mitcham Chess Club—in about 1996. I had written a slightly scurrilous club bulletin since 1981 and club colleagues always seemed to enjoy my stuff, even though I spent most of my time taking the mickey out of them. So the Web looked like a good way to get a bigger audience, and the technology seemed so straightforward and cheap. Later I set up the original 4NCL Website and then Britbase, which has a claim to be the first national online games archive (though there were already international ones and TWIC, of course). Those sites certainly got me noticed and led me to where I am today.

Did you have any technical problems?

Not especially. I was a computer programmer from 1978 to about 1987, so I am used to working with computers. On the Web it is usually possible to get hold of freeware which will fit the bill. I experimented with various free Web editors, and only paid money for a good one long after the 4NCL site was well established. Anyway, I am not very interested in flashy technical material; text, diagrams and a few photographs are enough for me.

You cover a wide range of subjects on the BCM, BCF and Britbase sites, but what are your own personal interests—what do you like reading?

I think that Britbase is my first love, although it is really an impossible task to collect so many British games. It stems from when I took up chess at school, and copied and collected scores of games in a ring binder. Using a chess database is great, and appeals to the archivist in me (another job I would have liked to get into). Of all the aspects of chess and chess-playing, it is probably chess history that I enjoy the most, though I wouldn't claim to be especially knowledgeable about it.

What material can people find on your sites that they can't find in magazines and books?

The minutiae of British chess and obscure British game scores from the past. They can often find this material on my Websites first; although other magazines, Websites and newspapers will inevitably use the raw material soon afterwards. There is no copyright on game scores or sports results, so one gets used to seeing other people reuse one's own work. Other things that people can find on my sites are *quality data* and an *independent voice*—neither of these commodities can be taken for granted in the chess media or on the Web. The chess world has become increasingly polarised, but I try to be even-handed.

Do you think that Internet chess clubs will gradually supplant real chess clubs? Do you play chess on the Internet—if so, where?

Chess is like sex—it is only healthy when it involves two consenting humans in the same room. Seriously, I've tried Internet chess and can understand why some people like it—but it's not for me and I hope that it doesn't supplant 'terrestrial chess'. That said, the Web has been a fantastic way for chess players the world over to get to know each other and become a truly global community; I'm thinking more of Websites and e-mail contacts than playing Internet chess. But nothing can beat seeing your mates at the chess club and having a beer with them after the match.

In 1999 you took over as editor of the British Chess Magazine (BCM) and immediately began work on their Website. What effect did that have on your existing Websites and your contribution to them?

In fact I started work on the BCM Website before becoming *BCM* editor in 1999. It was I who set it up from scratch to the specification of the then editor; and no one other than me has ever managed the site. When I became editor of the magazine, I moved the British news element of the 4NCL Website, and the Britbase archive, under the banner of the BCM. I resigned as 4NCL Web page editor at the same time; this was only ever a voluntary job, though I was occasionally paid some expenses. The material was mine and the Web server on which it resided, was paid for by me. Around the same time, Mitcham Chess Club sadly became defunct. Despite that, it still has a Website, where I occasionally publish nostalgia items purely for the entertainment of my former club colleagues.

A replacement 4NCL Website was set up by the 4NCL itself, for the publication of administrative details, contact information and results. I no longer contribute to it and it is for others to judge what effect my move to the BCM had on it. I still report on 4NCL news for BCM, of course, and provide a Web archive of previous seasons' results and games. As for Britbase, it has not developed as fast as I might have liked, due to my other responsibilities, but I still find time to publish new material there, including archive photographs from *British Chess Magazine*.

The British news section on the BCM Website is surely a key feature: is it easy to produce and has it added to the business BCM does via its Website?

It is certainly a key feature, and one that I enjoy very much. In some senses it is easy—I've been doing this sort of thing for a long time now and the technical side of it is straightforward— but there is more and more chess news appearing on the Web competing for an audience. It helps to supplement the big news stories and articles that we publish in the printed magazine. It is a very important factor in attracting business to the company. I don't see how a chess magazine could hope to compete without a supplementary Web-based news service these days.

BCM won the contract early in 2000 to publish *ChessMoves* and to run the BCF Website. Since then, the Website has vastly improved and *ChessMoves* is available online: how much of this has this been down to you?

The Web design and layout for the revamped BCF Website were carried out by me personally, to the content specification of the BCF. I built the initial set of pages, editing material from the inherited set-up as appropriate. Similarly, I drew up the layout for the online *ChessMoves* magazine and edited the initial June 2000 edition. John Emms and Syringa Turvey have since taken over day-to-day responsibility for editing the BCF Website and producing the online newsletter, and are doing a tremendous job.

Where do you get your material from? Is there anything you wouldn't publish?

In the early days my main provider was prolific British chess organiser Adam Raoof, so a special thank you to him. These days the *BCM* is a natural focus for chess information, which flows in from many sources. It is also good practice to 'network', and I try to keep in touch with the movers and shakers of the chess world. There are many helpful people in Britain and the rest of the world who are prepared to contribute to news gathering, or to assist with innovative projects such as Britbase—I'd like to take this opportunity to thank them all for their enormous help.

Old chess magazines, books and bulletins also provide a fund of interesting material to use, especially game scores, and I enjoy combing through them, looking for old material that could be of interest to modern readers. I wouldn't publish anything libellous, unsubstantiated, biased, personally offensive, sexist, or under copyright. I've been thinking of several facetious answers to this question, but the sensible side of my personality finally prevailed.

Who in particular helps you with the sites?

Indirectly, lots of people. I have listed all the people worldwide who have contributed to Britbase, who have provided material, encouragement and practical advice. These days my *BCM* and BCF colleagues give direct feedback on my Web writings and design.

How much time do you spend working on your sites? Does your wife complain?

With magazine responsibilities, I have tried to cut down how long I spend working on my Web pages. But it probably still comes to about three or four hours a day, often long into the night. Elaine is an angel who never complains about anything. She knows that, "a man's gotta do what a man's gotta do".

How much feedback do you get from visitors to your sites and what are their main criticisms/aspects that they particularly like?

People generally say very kind things about what I've been doing, and give lots of encouragement. I can't think of any significant criticisms, although omissions from the tournament calendar can sometimes irritate organisers; and I occasionally get ticked off for things like not mentioning little Jimmy winning the Under-8's grading prize at the Trumpton Junior Rapidplay—usually by Little Jimmy's mum.

What has been your greatest scoop?

I can't think of anything significant. I briefly became the conduit through which flowed much vituperation between the UK and Austria a few years ago, when an Austrian match captain was alleged to have sworn at and abused a Slough player during the game. This was exciting for a while but became burdensome when some of the messages started to be flagrantly libellous.

Britbase continues to travel backwards in time: how far do you actually intend to realistically go back to, and is Britbase likely to see more news history rather than old tournament games to download?

In many ways the cut-off date of 1930 is an artificial one. I may as well take it back to the beginning of time. But I have yet to come across any complete tournaments from pre-1930 that haven't already been published, probably because I've never seen any bulletins from before that time. Chess history is a good area to get into, and of course helps to promote the *BCM*. In my view the magazine is the best English-language journal of chess historical record that there is, and I'm proud to be its current custodian. I shall continue to seek ways to make that record available to those interested in chess history.

Can both Britbase and the main BCM site continue to expand and be improved?

Of course. The only difficulty is finding the time and resources to expand and implement some of the ideas which I have for them.

Which Websites are your own personal favourites, and which do you consider to be rivals?

When I'm looking for international news, I visit all the usual sites including TWIC, KasparovChess, Inside Chess and Europe Echecs. Unfortunately, as with British newspapers, it is increasingly difficult to find chess news pages with a truly independent outlook. One of my particular favourites is the French site, Notzai, on the Web, which is presented in the form of daily diary entries, with links to current tournaments and obscure but interesting chess articles, all laced with dry, Gallic humour. I just wish my French was up to a full appreciation of Pascal Villalba's witticisms. I also visit many Spanish and South American sites. This helps to form a well-balanced picture of what is happening in the chess world. It can be surprising to find how different their take on events can be.

When I'm looking for chess articles to read, I go to The Chess Café, which has a plethora of good article writers and reviewers. As regards British sites, I'm very fond of Richard Haddrell's SCCU site, which is regularly updated with news, unfussily presented, and tells it like it is. When I'm looking for links, I go to the New in Chess site, which has the best and most up-to-date selection of chess links in every conceivable category.

As regards rivals, anyone who sells chess books and equipment via the Web is a rival, but it is normal and acceptable to have professional business rivalries. I am rather more bothered by amateur chess Webmasters who put links to international online booksellers on their club sites for what must be a few, derisory pennies. This isn't a big problem— yet. But people probably don't realise the potential damage to specialist chess businesses. Every penny that goes to the big battalions goes out of chess (and Britain) forever, with the grim prospect of a world with no specialist chess retailers or magazines. Here's an analogy: try and imagine how the shopkeeper in your local corner grocer's would react if the front window of everyone's house in the road suddenly sported a 'Shop at Tesco's' poster...

B/ Websites

1) Batsford Chess ***
www.batsford.com/Chess/index.html

Headers: *Feedback, Bookclub, Bargain Books, Shopping, Search, Trade, Corporate, Chess Suppliers, Subject Catalogue*

Pricecheck: *Batsford's Modern Chess Openings £19.99/Bookclub members' price £16.99, Genius in Chess £12.99/Bookclub members' price £11.04*

A rather bland site which doesn't really make you want to buy direct from the publisher. The homepage consists of a picture of the covers of new works along with a small blurb about them. Clicking on a cover, in the hope of finding more, merely brings up the same information but this time filling the screen. The links page and list of chess suppliers are quite good (although surely Batsford would prefer you to buy direct from them), unlike the chess catalogue, which brings up a list of all chess books in print in a random order.

The main benefit of the site is that you can join the Batsford book club free online and then enjoy a 15 per cent discount on all books. Sadly, since this site was redesigned, following the Chrysalis takeover of Batsford, many good features, such as the personality profiles of authors, have vanished, but hopefully they will return. This site may also improve, as soon as Batsford return to regularly bringing out high-quality works.

2) BCM Online *****
www.bcmchess.co.uk

Headers: *What's New, Books, Software, Reviews, Computers, Sets & Boards, Videos, Equipment, Calendar,*

Magazine Subscription, What's in the Magazine, Britbase, Order from BCM, Bound Volumes, How to Find Us, Map, Second-Hand

Pricecheck: Play the Open Games as Black £15.99 (plus p&p, 10 per cent UK and 20 per cent overseas), Fritz6 £37.99+£2.50 p&p, Annual subscription to British Chess Magazine £30.00 (UK), £32.00 (Europe Airfreight), £37.00 (Europe Airmail), £36.50/US$60.00 (Rest of the World Airfreight), £44.50 /$73.00 Rest of the World Airmail)

This site has improved significantly since Webmaster John Saunders took over as *British Chess Magazine* editor in May 1999. One highlight is the main page, which is split in two, with all the new books and software along with the latest *BCM* displayed on the left and chess news on the right. This is the best source of UK chess news anywhere, even better than the recently improved BCF Website, with weekend tournament reports and daily updates on UK international events. There is also an excellent UK tournament calendar, although in contrast the coverage of overseas events is rather poor.

The site could still perhaps do with a few more graphics, but more importantly it is easy to use. Basic information on each new title is available just by clicking on the book's cover, and once it has been reviewed in *BCM* itself, you can read the review, usually of a good standard, online. Along with the wide range of software and books available, the BCM Website is also home to Britbase and the homepage of Gambit, the publishing company owned by Murray Chandler, John Nunn and Graham Burgess. This lists all their publications, but rather arbitrarily. For the more recent releases there is a little information about each book, whereas for some of the older ones, there are merely quotations from reviews of them— surely a mixture of the two for each book would be best.

3) Chess City ****
www.chesscity.com
Headers: *Analysis, Books, Fun, History, News, Resources, Whiz Kids*

Pricecheck: *Hypermodern Opening Repertoire for White US$16.95, Whiz Kids Teach Chess $14.95*

This popular site serves not only as a front for publisher Avery Cardoza's works, but also for Eric Schiller's analysis and articles. Information about all Cardoza's books can be found, and they can apparently be ordered by clicking on the picture of their cover, but at the time of writing this usually failed to work. Good use is made of Adobe Acrobat 3.0, which loads automatically, enabling you to read sample chapters before deciding on which works to purchase. Elsewhere on the site there is something for everyone, ranging from the latest gossip to some serious 19th-century history. Schiller also annotates several games, which can be downloaded; and in various forums, such as one on unorthodox openings, responds to readers' queries.

You can also read about his bizarre experience at a concert by the innovative pop group Phish, when a giant chessboard appeared on stage; or, if it is up your street, view a copy of the 1984 USSR v Rest of the World match's special menu, autographed by Ray Keene. Sadly the spelling is not perfect everywhere, whilst the site does generally seem to be easier and quicker to navigate with Netscape than with Internet Explorer.

4) Chess Informant ****
www.sahovski.co.yu

Headers: *Latest News, Online Shop, Distributors*

Pricecheck: Chess Informant 78 *(electronic or printed edition) £19.90/US$36.00,* Encyclopaedia of Openings E, 3rd ed. *(electronic edition) £19.80/$32.40 approx.,* E32-39 Nimzo-Indian *(printed edition) £6.90/$10.48 approx. (all plus 10 per cent for registered mail delivery or 30 per cent for airmail delivery)*

Chess Informant still sees the top players annotating the latest games, and its Belgrade publisher now produces virtually everything in both electronic and hard-copy form. The 'Chess Informant Reader' can be downloaded and then used to play through the games and analysis in the electronic books, providing that you can manage to unzip the download. When you register your free copy, you become a member of the Chess Informant Internet Club, and receive two free electronic publications, as well enjoying a 25 per cent discount on printed books in the online shop. Here all Chess Informant products can be purchased, and there is a useful link to a real-time currency converter, so that you can find the current price in your own currency.

Sadly the Chess Informant Chess School is not as good as the rest of the site and, despite having been founded in 1999, it still contained only the basic rules at the time of writing. Hopefully this situation will improve, whilst there are also plans, depending upon readers' feedback, to introduce online playing to the site.

5) Chess Mail *****
www.chessmail.com

Headers: *John Elburg's reviews, About Chess Mail, Site Map, What's new, Virus warning, Search tips, Oriental games,* Copper Wire *by Robert Harding*

Pricecheck: *Basic annual subscription to* Chess Mail UK *£28.00 (UK)/44 euros/IR£34.65 (Europe Airmail), US$60.00/ 50 euros/IR£39.35 (North America and rest of the world*

Airmail), Mega Corr CD (by normal mail) IR£20.00 (approx. $24.00)

There is plenty to find here for both correspondence and non-correspondence players. A range of interesting sample articles will probably make you want to subscribe to *Chess Mail*, whilst there are thousands of games available for download. These include 400 by the late Latvian GM Aivars Gipslis, and there is also a fine obituary of him. Should you want a change from the chess, then there is an introduction to several oriental board games, as well as two fascinating extracts from *Copper Wire*, a book by Harding's father about his experiences as a World War II fighter pilot and German POW. Elsewhere the book reviews by Harding and John Elburg are of a high standard, and there are many recent tournaments results to peruse, plus links to every imaginable CC site on the Web.

6) Chess Mentor ****
www.chess.com/home.html
Headers: *About Us, Products, Support, Free Demo, How to Buy, Play Chess Online, Search, Reviews & Endorsements, Customer Feedback, FAQs, Dealer List, System Requirements, Search*

Pricecheck: *Chess Mentor—Basic Chess Course US$49.95, Chess Mentor for Advanced Players $79.95, both plus $7.50 shipping & handling (domestic) or $15.00 (international), and 8.25 per cent sales tax for California residents*

A demo version of the Chess Mentor software can be downloaded here and it is a persuasive advertisement. Users learn by active participation and experiment, and are given various challenge positions to solve. Themes connected to each challenge are explained, whilst the program swiftly analyses your results, producing a score and picking out which positions need to be revisited and reassessed.

There is, however, no option to play against the program, which solely acts as a coach and guide. There are several different levels of course available, with the coaching tips provided by a strong team of US coaches, headed by IM Jeremy Silman. The large amount of positive feedback displayed on the site emphasises that Chess Mentor is innovative, fun and easy to use.

7) Gambit-Soft *****
www.gambitsoft.com/gambit1e.htm
Headers: *News, Chess Programs, Chess Databases, Chess Tutorials, Chess Shareware/Freeware, Chess Demos, Upgrades and Patches, Utilities, Problem Chess, PC chess*

boards and other material, Chess Computer Tournaments, FAQ, Pricelist, MAC programs, Guestbook, Bargain Sales!!!

Pricecheck: *Fritz6 US$52.00, Chess Assistant5 with Tiger Engine $150.00, Rebel Century $52.00*

Practically every chess-related computer program under the sun is for sale at this site belonging to the German company, Gambit-Soft, and many are discounted (check out the Bargain Sales!!! section for the latest offers). There are over a hundred free small programs, such as engines for Winboards, to download, whilst the news section provides all the latest information about new products and the tournament performances of playing programs. Many of the reviews are quite detailed, and Mac owners will find the page devoted to short descriptions of, and links to, Mac chess software very helpful.

8) Inside Chess *****
www.insidechess.com

Headers: *Products, Chess Articles, Events, E-mail Subscription List, Masterpiece Inc., ICE-Store, Chess.net*

Pricecheck: *The Unknown Bobby Fischer US$18.95/Dfl42.30/DM 34.90/£15.00, plus $4.50 regular shipping (US), PerfectBase 1996 $45.00 plus $6.75 regular shipping (US), Yasser Seirawan's Chess Timer $11.95 plus $2.25 regular shipping (US)*

Inside Chess is sadly no longer available in printed form, but it continues to produce monthly high-quality articles which can be found here. Particular highlights are GM Yasser Seirawan's views on the chess world, Edward Winter attacking Eric Schiller's "mendacity", IM Jeremy Silman's reviews and detailed theoretical articles by IM Zoran Ilic. Seirawan's International Chess Enterprises, Inc. also provide an online shop, and although the number of books available is not large, excerpts from them are often available, which certainly assists the purchaser. You can also buy books from Seirawan's personal library, or the portable chess timer he invented for kids with small wallets.

9) Internet Chess Academy **
www.totalchess.com

Headers: *Take the Tour!, Member Login*

Pricecheck: *Join the ICA US$9.95 per month*

Gaby Baby, as GM Gabriel Schwartzman has been cruelly nicknamed, is a former child prodigy-turned columnist and lecturer. Schwartzman asks for almost $10 a month, which is about twice as much as a subscription to a chess magazine, for two fairly simplistic and general lectures, two puzzles and a short column each week. There is so much good chess tutorial material available elsewhere on the Internet for free, that Schwartzman needs to put in much more effort to make his services value for money. If you're looking for lectures, simuls and the opportunity to observe GM games, skip Schwartzman and go to the Internet Chess Club. Also beware of the free tour, which is packed full of clever advertising language and makes the site out to be far better than it is.

10) London Chess Centre ****
www.chesscenter.com
Headers: *TWIC, Online Shop, Openings, Bridge, TWIC TV, Kingpin, Chess Auction, Fantasy Chess, Chess Shop, New Software, Chessbase7, New Books, Book Archive, New Products, Full Booklist, Luxury Sets, Decorative Sets, Downloads, Go, Backgammon, Book Reviews*

Pricecheck: *Annual subscription to* CHESS *£34.95 (UK), £44.95 (Europe), US$70.00 (USA & Canada, by Airspeed 2nd class), $100.00 (Rest of World Airmail), $80.00 (Rest of World Surface Mail), Fritz6 £39.95 plus £4.00 (UK)/£5.99 (Europe by Air)/£9.99 (Rest of World by Swift Air),* Batsford's Modern Chess Openings *£19.99/$29.99*

The emporium on Euston Road has a decent Website offering plenty of products and a number of special features. There is a direct link to 'Fantasy Chess', the chess equivalent of fantasy football, whilst the sample articles of *Kingpin*, the leading satirical chess magazine, are very enjoyable. Live coverage and commentary on a few selective events, such as the British Championships, is hosted on the site, and you can stay updated with the LCC's latest arrivals and international tournament news by joining the weekly free newsletter. IM John Watson's superb and detailed book reviews are available, but the complete book list consists of just one long list of titles. Fortunately there is a little information about new products, but it would be nice to be able to see a good search facility in the online shop.

11) New in Chess ****
www.newinchess.com
Headers: *Products, Shop, Reviews, Service*

Pricecheck: *Annual subscription to* New in Chess *Magazine Dfl95.00 (Holland), £42.00/57.52 euros/DM112.99 (Europe), US$78.00 (USA & Rest of the World Airmail),* The King *Dfl120.00/54.55 euros/$55.00 plus Dfl4.50 (Holland)/13.50 euros (Europe)/$6.00 (USA) shipping costs*

The world's leading chess magazine has a correspondingly slick Website. Of course, New in Chess is not just a magazine, but also a publishing company which brings out high-quality books and CDs, including the NiC Yearbook, relied on by professional players. Other than the online shop, there is a superb range of over 2,000 links, whilst the reviews are, on the whole, very objective. Games from each magazine, albeit in unannotated form, can be downloaded. It would be nice to see some articles brightening up the site, to fully make one want to subscribe to the magazine.

12) Polgarchess **
www.polgarchess.com

Headers: *What's New?, Career Highlights, Chess Center, Queen of the Kings Game, Chess Shop, The Sisters' Events, Polgar Annotates, Simuls, Lectures, Private Lessons, Photo Directory, Current Events*

Pricecheck: *Polgar Chess Authority Club Membership US$120.00 a year ($90.00 for juniors/seniors), Plastic Chess Set (Staunton Style) $8.95, Encyclopaedia of Openings E $33.95, both plus a maximum of 14 per cent shipping & handling*

A messy hotch-potch of a site from former Women's World Champion Susan Polgar and her husband Jacob Shutzman, who are based in New York where they run a chess school and shop. The homepage certainly needs tidying, as new articles are stuck on randomly, along with the latest news on Polgar's court case against FIDE over her Women's World Championship title. There is a lack of sample material which would make you want to join the Polgar Chess Authority Club, and the monthly annotated games ceased in June 1998.

Most of the site, such as the playing schedule of the three Polgar sisters, is hopelessly out of date, and one wonders whether the online Chess Shop only receives books and software at least one year after they are produced, as there is a dearth of 1999 and 2000 publications. Possibly, as Polgar's baby son grows up, she may update the site and then a few visitors might start to consider forking out the minimum fee of $5,000 that she charges for a simul.

13) Rebel *****
www.rebel.nl/edindex.htm

Headers: *Rebel Board, Rebel price list, Dealer phone list, Dealer email list, How to order, Download Software, Playing Strength, Rebel vs Anand, Rebel vs Yusupov, Rebel subscribe, Rebel reviews, Rebel FAQ, Rebel at AEGON, EPD to diagrams, J Noomen Column, DIAZ Column, Rebel Decade, Company Profile, Cartoon mode*

Pricecheck: *Rebel Century* *US$59.95/59.00 euros/Dfl119.00, Rebel 10 $29.95/29.00 euros/Dfl59.00*

This homepage of the very strong computer program 'Rebel', boasts a vast amount of information relevant to the program. The layout could perhaps be a little more user-friendly, but it is hard to think of anything missing. Existing Rebel users will find answers to their problems as well as frequent upgrades, whilst Rebel Century owners have the option to join 'Rebel Subscribe' and receive the latest GM games to update their databases each month.

Potential Rebel buyers will find a host of reviews, hundreds of sample games to download, and best of all, Rebel Decade 3.0 (apparently identical to *Rebel 10,* other than being 200 Elo points weaker)—one of the many free downloads. Amongst the wide range of interesting tournament reports, excellent cartoons by Diaz, and articles, is a debate on how to make chess programs stronger, and reports on Rebel's match victories over Anand and Yusupov. Rebel users who wish to incorporate diagrams into text files will find the EPD2diag program useful.

14) SmartChess Online ****
www.smartchess.com
Headers: *Chess Superstore, Feature Product, SmartChess Online, Feature Article*

Pricecheck: Encyclopaedia of Chess Openings Volume E *US$32.00, Vinyl Board (Brown) & Club Special Set Value Pack $12.90, Fritz6 $47.50*

More than just a chess superstore, SmartChess Online has a mission statement: "To promote our royal game with vision, and on a grander scale than ever before imagined in America." Leading on from this they have supported Irina Krush, possibly because they aim "to do everything in [their] power to create an American World Chess Champion", whose homepage is part of the site, as are Anatoly Karpov's and Alexei Shirov's. SmartChess Online! is published every month, and consists mainly of news and reports on Irina Krush's activities, although there is also other American tournament news and game annotations by GM Ron Henley. Elsewhere, no less a player than Anatoly Karpov, assists in clearly explaining the moves, whilst clubs can join the 'SmartClub Program' and thus entitle their members to special offers and discounts. The range of products for sale is very large, although there is a dearth of detailed information about most—books are at best described by their back-cover blurb.

15) Tigerchess ****
www.checkerwise.co.uk

> Headers: *Secure Shopping, Chess Training, Events & Seminars, Articles by GM Davies, Problems, Book Guide*
>
> Pricecheck: *Game Assessment £55.00 for five games, Telephone Coaching £20.00 per half hour, The Power Chess Program: Book 2 £16.99, Albin Counter Gambit (video) £15.99 + £1.00 p&p*
>
> GM Nigel Davies offers a wide range of coaching services, especially his evening and weekend seminars in Manchester, and this site acts as a good front for them. Davies presents an interesting questionnaire for surfers to see if they are chessboard tigers (should they want to know), whilst his weekly columns and the superb 'grandmaster growl' provide interesting viewpoints on the life of a professional and on coaching.
>
> There is also a guest section by IM Andrew Martin, who, like Davies, is an enthusiastic author, featuring some interesting opening analysis, which can either be downloaded or viewed with the replayable game window (for which either Internet Explorer 4, Netscape Navigator 4.0, or a more recent version of them is required, as is the case with all the games on this site). The wide array of problems available should challenge and inspire, and if you were wondering which books to study, then Davies' recommendations of many classics should prove helpful.

16) Your Move Chess and Games ****
www.icdchess.com

> Headers: *Chess Pieces, Chess Sets, Chess Boards, Chess Software, Chess Tables, Chess Computers, Tournament Supplies, Chess Books, Chess Clocks, Internet Specials, Mail Order Policies*
>
> Pricecheck: *Fritz6 US$48.95, Tudor Kings and Queens Crushed Stone Chess Pieces $169.95, Play the Open Games as Black $20.36 (all plus Shipping, Handling and Insurance Charges)*
>
> This shop in New York offers a fairly large selection of chess products and all sorts of other games, including Go, Shogi, Chinese Checkers, and Gambling Supplies. The selection of many different sets and boards, including hundreds of different themed chess pieces, is excellent, and these are well illustrated with photographs. 'Your Move' is, however, not so strong on books, but does have a good selection of software and descriptions of the various programs, with links to the latest computer ratings to help you make your choice.

9
Miscellaneous

Some of the most imaginative sites can't be easily categorized. These include The Chess Show, a crazy cable TV show; The Chess Variant Pages, for people who find ordinary chess too easy; and Randy's Revealing Reviews, one of the best sites on the Web for book reviews. In this chapter you'll also find the home pages of various players, famous and not-so-famous; chess links sites; correspondence chess sites; chess teaching material; and a plethora of poorly-attended newsgroups.

A/ Webmaster Hall of Fame

John C. Knudsen, The Correspondence Chess Place

Please introduce yourself

I'm John C. Knudsen, born in Iowa, USA, a little over 44 years ago. I joined the Army in 1973 (Reserves) and went on active duty in 1974. I spent 20 years and two days in the Army, 'retiring' as a Chief Legal Noncommissioned Officer (E-7) in 1994. The civilian equivalent to this would be a law office manager, I think. Since 1995, I have been employed by the

Army in Europe as a Department of Defense civilian employee. I work in Mannheim, Germany. My family and I live in a small town, Osthofen, which is about 50km away from Mannheim.

Do you play over-the-board chess?

I was very active in chess as a teenager in Iowa; well, all around the midwestern United States. I am a 'Fischer Baby', having taught myself the moves and the games during the 1972 Fischer-Spassky match. What I soon discovered was that, try as I might, my over-the-board chess was, well, pathetic. I think my highest over-the-board rating was 1850-1900, very bad really. Due to work and family problems, I started concentrating on correspondence chess in 1978. I found that I could raise my level of play two or three classes in CC. After that, I was hooked. For many years, my skill level in CC hovered round the expert level, but, in 1998, I finally achieved Master, in the Correspondence Chess League of America (CCLA); and in April 2000, I achieved a 2418 rating in the International Correspondence Chess Federation (ICCF).

I now devote my playing exclusively to the master (and higher) level. There are many talented players and it is always a challenge to do well against them. Of course, with my many other responsibilities it is somewhat hard to carry much of a game level nowadays. I now lean towards fewer games going at one time, but much more effort concentrated in those games.

So does this mean you don't have to be a strong over-the-board player to be a strong CC player?

It is possible to be a strong CC player and weak over-the-board player—such players are called 'Correspondence Chess Specialists'. Usually however, strong CC players are also strong crossboard players—probably at least master strength. It is hard to compare the two forms of the game—and I cannot explain why some players can play two or three levels higher in CC. Part of it is the research factor, no doubt; but the most important difference is the reflection time. I might spend 100-200 hours of analysis on an important or difficult game—the level of play is bound to be raised with that kind of study. No one likes to play poor chess. One of the main attractions of CC for me is that often I can play a master quality game. In over-the-board chess, the limited reflection time shows in the number of gross blunders I produce.

When and why did you decide to set up a Website?

In the summer of 1996 I noticed that there wasn't very much coverage of correspondence chess on the World Wide Web. It was then I decided to give it a whirl, to see what I could do in this area.

Did you have any technical problems?

Many, many problems at the beginning. Teaching myself HTML, the mechanics of setting up an attractive Website, etc. Most of my technical problems were caused by my lack of knowledge and stupidity. Everything I have learned, I have taught myself or learned from others. Along the way I have learned much from my many friends who keep me straight and help me. I had done some previous writing for some small US CC magazines, so the desire to write was always a big motivating factor. There is just so much garbage being published on the World Wide Web! A good example of this is the recent 'Frequently Asked Questions' (FAQ) file being circulated on the *rec.games.chess.play-by-email* newsgroup. The ICCF, which totally dominates international correspondence chess (both postal and e-mail) is listed almost dead last in the list of e-mail correspondence chess organisations! Ignorance/deliberate snubbing such as this is unfortunate, because it gives new and potential CC players the wrong impression—the end result being they would waste their time with 'low rent' organisations, instead of starting out in legitimate, official correspondence chess. I felt that there was a need for correspondence chess players from all over the world to have a place they could call home, hence the original name, The Correspondence Chess Place (TCCP). TCCP has now grown into the domain: *correspondencechess.com/net/org*, which is a hub of sites devoted to correspondence chess. Another primary motivation was to give something back to the game that had brought me so much satisfaction. I started out very small and things have just grown from there. I am quite happy with the progress we have made down this road. But we have a long way to go...

Were there any particular disasters, say when you deleted big chunks of material or put something on the site that shouldn't have been there?

I have deleted files by mistake and had to re-do them. I had an ISP delete my entire site by mistake one time! And the backups, too! Luckily, a couple of weeks before that I had purchased a zip drive and backed up my entire site. Needless to say, I am a firm believer in backing up my site (and all other sites hosted at my site). There was also an incident when I published some true anecdotes about a CC organisation that I used to be involved with. This resulted in me being threatened with a civil suit and I decided, rather than risk the time and expense of a lengthy legal battle, to pull the material from my pages.

Where do you get your material from and do you pay contributors?

Quite a bit of the material comes from the limited brain matter contained in my head; the rest comes from friends and others who contribute. I have paid contributors for material, but, as this has always been a boot-strap adventure, I haven't been able to attract all of the big talent that I would wish to. Tenth US Correspondence Chess Champion, Jon Edwards, has been a staunch supporter from the humble start and throughout all of this. The same goes for my good friend, International Master Tim Harding from Ireland. And I credit the American journalist, J. Franklin Campbell, with much of the support and inspiration for my site. We are very good friends. There are just so many people to acknowledge...

When you refer to 'big talent', who in particular do you wish would contribute to your site?
What are your criteria for good material, and is there anything that you wouldn't publish because you find it too uninteresting or too controversial?

Big talent for me would be world CC champions, world FIDE champions, and so forth. GM Penrose is an incredible CC player, and, of course, I would love to publish anything by a player of that calibre! Any old master can perform analysis. What I am looking for are the behind-the-scenes insights for the average player. What is going on in the master's mind, if you like. Players want to read about CC, as well as play it. I am very discriminating about what I will publish. I won't publish any material that is not suitable for older children, for example. I detest politics, and especially chess politics, so I try and stay away from pieces by players with an agenda other than the game. Of course, one must always avoid publishing copyrighted material without adequate permissions.

Does the Website make a profit for you from sales of books and software?

Interesting question. I have sunk thousands of hours and thousands of dollars into the development of my site, advertising, etc. Any commercial activity on the site is meant to help the site become self-supporting and grow. Between banner advertising and donations, we are squeaking by...

How much feedback do you get from readers, and what are their main criticisms/aspects that they particularly like?

I get a lot of feedback from readers. They generally like my common man approach to correspondence chess, and my enthusiasm about what it offers to every player. It is funny, but I usually inspire hatred from about five per cent, and support from the other 95 per cent. The five per cent I ignore, and the 95 per cent I cultivate.

What sort of things do people say?

Being a Webmaster is often a lonely thing. I've gotten hate e-mails from people who are either jealous of me or are just plain nuts. Things that can't be repeated here. Once on the TCCMB (The Correspondence Chess Message Board), a poster called me an idiot—someone who wanted to be a somebody but was in fact a nobody. You can't pay attention to these (usually unnamed) types of posts or e-mails. I have received compliments from many grandmasters (both over-the-board and CC) but the ones that mean the most to me are the regular players who credit me with a rekindled (or new) interest in CC. Promotion of CC is what it is all about. The result is more CC players.

Do you think the Website has inspired many people to start playing CC, who otherwise wouldn't have considered it?

I know it has. It is the thing that pleases me the most about this endeavour.

What surprises newcomers most about CC when they delve into it? What are their most common preconceptions?

Good question. The first preconceived notion that some strong over-the-board players have is that they will be very strong CC players! Not necessarily so—they are used to most opponents blundering against them soon in their over-the-board chess and are often surprised when CC players play well against them. For novices, the required record keeping seems overwhelming at first, but once they become more experienced, it just becomes part of the game. Many players who have not tried CC, feel that everyone uses a computer to generate their moves—this is a false generalization. At the master level and higher in CC, you would hope that your opponent is using a computer program! The programs now available, fail badly at the higher levels.

What difference has e-mail made to CC?

E-mail has made a tremendous difference in CC. With postal CC, the most common complaint has always been the transit time for the mail, particularly to and from Eastern Europe and Cuba. In international CC, sometimes a Tournament Secretary would require registered mail transmission of moves—very cheap for Eastern Europe and very expensive in the West. Now, with e-mail CC, there is little or no transit time problem.

These are exciting times for CC, largely because of the e-mail medium. Of course, with e-mail, there is a tendency to shoot off a move quicker than one normally would. That is the only area of concern that I see. The duration of games (in months/years) is shorter, but the reflection time is basically the same. That is a direct result of little or no transit time. Some still prefer snail mail CC (I don't!), and this form of CC will be around for quite a while. I have a theory about this, though. Traditional snail mail CC clubs/organisations who don't get in on the e-mail bandwagon, will eventually either die out as being no longer necessary, or become nothing more than pen-pal clubs.

What are your future plans for the site?

No secrets will be given away here! I have a reputation for trying out new ideas. Innovation is a necessary thing to make a mark in the business. Sometimes I wake up in the middle of the night with a new idea, and later on give it a try. It is all about finding your niche and then going for it. Since correspondencechess.com already attracts tens of thousands of visitors a month, keeping the site interesting is a major task. The network of friends that I mentioned above keeps me focused on the right things, which makes this task a much simpler one. I aim to provide the worldwide CC community with *the* place to go, to enjoy our form of the game.

Which are your favourite chess Websites and why?

I am partial to correspondence chess sites, for obvious reasons. The ICCF site; Tim Harding's Chess Mail site; as well as J. Franklin Campbell's The Campbell Report. Campbell in particular has this ability to attract outstanding writers, and his own writing is quite excellent, in my opinion. That is the reason he is hosted at correspondencechess.com!

In what way does the purpose of The Correspondence Chess Place differ from the Campbell Report? In other words, why should people visit both sites?

Well, Campbell is a better writer than I am (although I do have my moments) and he is able to attract some of the best writers in the CC world. The Campbell Report and The Correspondence Chess Place are two totally different sites, his site is hosted at my site. I tend to have a broad view of where my site is headed. The bigger picture is that the site will be the first (and best) choice for the novice and experienced CC player to go, a place where he or she feels comfortable to be. We have gone a long way towards that goal—but, and this is an important but, any sub-site (for lack of a better term) hosted by me, is totally independent, without any editorial control on my part. No one gets hosted by me unless they meet my definition of excellence. What that exact definition is, I'll keep to myself, but anyone with an obvious love for CC and the desire to impart that enthusiasm to the CC world would be highly desired. The ultimate goal is for correspondencechess. com to be the 'home' for a number of outstanding sites like Campbell's.

I mentioned before that you have to find your niche and go with it. Since the first edition of this book, we have added several sites to correspondencechess.com. These include 10th World Correspondence Chess Champion Vytas (Victor) Palciauskas' The World of Correspondence Chess; International Arbiter Ralph Marconi's Chess Page; The Canadian Correspondence Chess Association (CCCA); American Postal Chess Tournaments (APCT); and The Chess Journalists of America (CJA) site. We've been busy! We now dominate the correspondence chess niche on the Web— between 30,000 and 40,000 hits per month. No one else is even close...

A big draw continues to be The Correspondence Chess Message Board (TCCMB)—it is already the premier forum for CC players on the Web. We have grandmasters and novices rubbing shoulders side-by-side, discussing issues and concerns essential to the CC player—it is a great resource. And the archive containing all the postings can be easily stored for future reference (or offline reading). Another fantastic resource. You want to learn about CC—read that archive!

B/ Best of the Web

Chess Tips

There's nothing better for a player's confidence than to obtain a position that they understand and just 'know' how to play. A player whose repertoire regularly leads to these types of positions will be a formidable opponent.

While I think that opening theory, for the average player, is over-rated and over-utilized, I believe that this study, if done properly, can be beneficial. I'm going to explain how I used study of one defense to become a better chess player.

My basic premise is that for a player to truly 'own' a defense, they must use that defense as a vehicle to expand their overall chess knowledge. This will require a real chess investment—much preparation, time, and effort will be required. However, the payoff can be significant.

I think that the player that puts in the time and effort required will become a better chess player. They will be better not only in the opening but in other stages as well, because to truly 'know' their defense they will have to learn a lot about middlegames and endgames along the way.

The defense that I like to call 'mine' is the Pirc Defense. I have been playing it for 20 years, and I can probably count the truly awful positions I've obtained from it on one (OK, maybe two...) hand(s). I've played it against grandmasters, international masters, masters, experts, and class players. I have a decent plus score with it against players rated over 2200 and a strong plus score against players rated over 2000. It has served me very well over the years.

One of the benefits of truly 'knowing' a defense is that, once you've built a solid foundation, it takes much less work to maintain it. I also play the Sicilian Defense, and I spend much more time on it than I do on the Pirc, even though these days I usually reserve the Pirc for my strongest opponents. I've done so much work in the past on this defense that I feel confident in my ability to work positions out at the board.

What follows are some steps I would suggest for a player seeking to make a present defense 'their' defense. I would offer a couple of caveats. First, one must already have at least a general knowledge of a defense before embarking on this program. You have to already have the basics in place. Second, you should be sure that the defense you're going to invest all this time and effort in is worth the trouble. In other words, make sure it's really the line you want to play (at least some of the time) for a long time.

Gather And Catalogue Information

When I started playing, computers were definitely not in the typical home. To collect my chess information, I used a big loose-leaf, three-ring binder. I got lots of notebook paper, dividers (to separate variations within the defense), and dividers with pockets to hold photocopied articles or other things that I wanted to keep stored.

Even though I now own three computers, I still have my loose-leaf, three-ring Pirc binders. There are now about three of them, and I still take them to tournaments with me sometimes. If you don't have a computer (and even if you do), I would suggest that you start in this less technological way.

Later (or sooner, if you're adept at using the computer for chess study), you can do the same things (and more) on the computer that you can do with your binder. One program that's quite useful for developing your repertoire is Bookup. I've used it for several years and think quite highly of it.

Find A Role Model

To really understand how to play a defense, you need to find a strong player (the stronger the better) whose games you can study. When I was growing up with the Pirc, there were a host of these players who regularly played it. I looked carefully at the games of Jan Timman, Vlastimil Hort, and Eugenio Torre. They were all world class grandmasters who made their living with the defense.

Gather as many games as you can find of these players, who use your defense. Look for annotated games by the players themselves. They will be especially helpful for understanding your defense. Play over these games—the whole game—and then, at the end, write a brief synopsis of the game. Why did Black (or White) win? What were the relevant features of the position? What plans did both sides create/attempt to create? What questions did you have, or moves didn't you understand? Also note any tactical or strategic tricks or maneuvers that were utilized in the game (i.e. minority pawn attack, exchange bishop for knight for pawn structure, sacrifice pawn for development, etc.). Put all of these in your notebook in the section on the specific variation of the defense.

Another useful exercise is to play solitaire chess with your role model's games (this works best with annotated games). You take the side of your role model, and cover up his/her moves. You make the move of the opponent and then seek to find the right move for your role model. After selecting your move, write it down and any supporting analysis, then uncover the move played and compare. If there are notes, compare them to your own thoughts. Then repeat this exercise with the remaining moves. This exercise will get you more involved in the game and also improve your analytical skills while you learn the opening.

Your goal here, of course, is greater understanding of the typical plans and play for both sides in the variations of your defense. As you acquire more and more of these games, you will start to see recurring themes, and, when you're confronted with positions in tournament games, you'll likely find the right move—even if you don't know that it is 'book'.

Tactics, Tactics, Tactics

As you disassemble and reassemble your defense, you'll be amazed how often the strategic ideas in a position are handled in a tactical fashion. You must grasp the recurring tactical themes in your defense. For example, anyone who plays the Accelerated Dragon Sicilian (1 e4 c5 2 ♘f3 ♘c6 3 d4 cxd4 4 ♘xd4 g6 5 ♘c3 ♝g7 6 ♝e3) knows that Black can often profit from playing ...d7-d5 in one go rather than playing d7-d6 and later advancing the pawn to d5. This is a recurring theme that Black must understand—both when it works and when it doesn't. Every defense has these, and you must search out games on your defense to find them.

When you do, write down the game (and create a diagram at the key point) and put it in your notebook. I kept a separate section for tactical themes and also cross-posted them in the section on the specific variation they came from. Review these regularly.

Fill In The Cracks

I took it for a given that you had already acquired at least one good book on your chosen defense. For starters, make sure that your primary book is a good one. Preferably, it has been written by a grandmaster or international master who actually plays the line in question. In the case of the Pirc, John Nunn, who was a regular Pirc practitioner in the 1980s, wrote a great book on the defense. Likewise, Kasparov has written about the Scheveningen Sicilian, Psahkis about the Benoni, Sveshnikov about the Pelikan Sicilian, Silman about the Accelerated Dragon, Watson about the French, etc.

The next step is to find secondary sources of information. Often you can find less well-known books written on 'your' defense. While I understand that budgets are limited, I would suggest that you acquire as many sources as possible on your key defenses. You'll often find that they list interesting alternatives that aren't considered in other texts. Go through those books and compare their recommendations to your other texts.

Inventory The Positions

By this time, you should have studied and analyzed games by key exponents of the line. You should have a solid book on the opening and perhaps some secondary sources, and you should have a listing of some key tactical and strategic themes, in the variations of 'your' defense. It's time to take stock.

It's time to create (either via computer software, books, or by hand) a repertoire—what it is you'll play against each of the major White tries against your defense. It's important that this be as concrete as possible for future reference. I used to write mine in pencil, with lots of spaces for changes, because your ideas will change as lines are played. Using your notebook allows you, of course, to insert or remove pages as necessary.

Once you've created your repertoire, you need to find a way to make sure that you really 'know' it. One of the more rewarding experiences for me, in terms of cementing my knowledge of my variation, was the opportunity to give a lecture at my local chess club about the Pirc Defense. This required that I distill into words the key ideas and themes of the defense and also structure the various methods for both sides to approach the positions. I spent a fair amount of time organizing the material and my thoughts. This was time well spent.

I would suggest that every player undertake that same exercise. Approach 'your' defense as if you were going to give a lecture on it to other chess players. Write it all down—the way that you would characterize the variations, the plans for both sides, the discussion of the specific variations. You'll be surprised at how well it inventories the variations and your thoughts.

You can do the same thing with another player. You can agree to lay out for another player the ideas and variations of one line in return for him/her doing the same with a different variation. I have done this with another strong player in the past, and we've both benefited.

Of course, all of this will go into your notebook!

Think For Yourself

By this time, between the study of games of strong players, sources of information on the defense, and inventorying the key aspects of the defense, you will have a good working knowledge of your defense. It's time to start making your own judgments about positions.

It's common for players to simply parrot the moves or suggestions of stronger players in the opening. However, if we're truly going to make an opening 'ours', we must get beyond this tendency. You have to believe in your line and be willing to take on published theory on occasion.

Optimize Use Of The Fruits Of Your Labor

One of the benefits of truly mastering an opening, is that you may be able to use the knowledge gained on the opposite side of the board. This would be possible, for example, for a player that plays the Sicilian as Black and 1 c4 as White. It also may be possible when a player is crazy enough to play 'your' variation against you.

Practice Regular Maintenance

Just as with your car or home, once you've invested the time and effort into your variation, don't forget to regularly 'check under the hood', so to speak. Check later publications (Informants, magazines, *Trends in the ...* etc.) for new developments. Continue to seek out strong players that are playing 'your' defense and study their games. And don't forget to learn typical endgames that arise from your defense. Shereshevsky and Slutsky have an excellent two-volume set,

Mastering the Endgame, that looks at endgames on the basis of the opening that they come from. In this way, you see how pawn structures and the middlegame plans for both sides shape the typical endgame. This would be a good starting point.

So, that's 'my' defense. Are you ready to get started on 'yours'?

Randy's Revealing Reviews
(http://ourworld.compuserve.com/ homepages/randybauer)

C/ Websites

1) Best Ukrainian chessplayer Vasyl' Ivanchuk's official page *
www.lvivchess.wertep.com/IVANCHUK/tivanchuk.shtml

Headers: *Ukraine Super Tournament of Category XVII, Workgroup*

Fans of Vasily Ivanchuk won't find much of a personal presence on this site. The player himself doesn't seem to have made any contribution. He neither writes nor coaches on the site, which was created by his admiring colleagues in Lviv. They provide tournament news in abysmal English: "Having phoned to Lviv Vasyl' Ivanchuk said that he is in a good mode and not disappointed with failures at the beginning of Linares-98 tournament. It have simply adversely affected the absense of playing practice on the highest level in the course of last 3 months." Ivanchuk has been rumoured to headbutt walls when he loses. If you spend too long trying to find anything worthy on this site... you will too.

2) Charlie's Chess Mess ****
home.earthlink.net/~pretendigm/index.html

Headers: *Chess Servers, Software, Pgn Games, Chess Mess Live*

A pity that Charlie won't reveal his identity: even when you download his best games played on the Internet Chess Club, there are no clues. Whoever and wherever he is, he has put in some hard work to provide visitors with a comprehensive range of software and PGN files, accompanied by a cosmic soundtrack that includes the *Mission Impossible* theme in all its synthesized glory. If you are looking for somewhere to play chess on the Internet or the software to play it with, this is the place to start. The PGN files are divided into grandmaster games (an impressive selection of players) and openings (also a wide choice).

3) Chess Corner *****
www.chesscorner.com

Headers: *Latest, Learn, Forum, Play, Games, Bookstore, Software, Fun, Chat, Champs, Baburin, UK, Clubs, Fun Section, Chess Internet Greeting Card, Chess Problems, Chess Quiz*

This friendly site has a little bit of everything for the chess enthusiast. Although many of the sections appear in other sites by the same author, this is well within both the spirit and the unwritten rules of the Internet. Besides, the site has a fun identity of its own. The Webmistress is teacher Janet Edwardson, who also runs a chess club in the real world. Maybe that's what makes the tutorial material for beginners look authoritative and fun. There is also an e-mail forum where you can leave messages and hopefully receive answers to your queries. If you are a beginner or have children interested in learning chess, then bookmark this excellent free service. It's all very bright and breezy, but there is also plenty of content for advanced players.

Britannica.com has awarded Chess Corner their Internet Guide Award for quality, accuracy of content, presentation and usability. Perhaps even more importantly, a glance at the update diary shows that the site is kept fresh. For example, the diary indicates that on Christmas Eve 1999, more clubs were added to the excellent UK Club Directory. Chess Corner has one of the best listings of chess software—Playing, Database, DTP and Web Design. It even has it's own Wireless Application Protocol (WAP) site (a mini version tailored for mobile phones). At the moment this WAP version of Chess Corner has only three pages, but more are sure to follow.

4) Chess is Fun *****
www.princeton.edu/~jedwards/cif/chess.html

Headers: *Introduction, Openings, Tactics, Endgames, Great Games, For Advanced Players, Attempted chess humor*

This is a superb place for learning about the game of chess or simply reading some entertaining articles. Each page is divided into two frames, so that you can keep a list of contents handy while you are looking at a particular item. The site is run by Jon Edwards, US correspondence chess champion, whose rating of 2470 is the highest ever obtained in American Postal Chess Tournaments history. It seems he's also an extremely good coach and an accomplished writer who knows his way around computers. What a show-off!

Apart from arranging the extensive contents list in a logical manner, so that you can easily find your way to an article on pawn chains or the Caro-Kann opening, Edwards supplies moving diagrams, so you don't have to bother getting a chessboard out. Great games from the past play themselves as you watch from the comfort of an armchair, with the score printed under the diagram. The same technique is used to illustrate the lessons—which is a great way to memorise how to mate with bishop and knight against king, for example. Edwards also offers a couple of columns with lengthy analysis for advanced players and some correspondence chess anecdotes.

5) Chess Graphics ****
www.cowderoy.com/graphics

Headers: *Cartoons, Ray tracing, Films, Pictures, Players, Pieces, Screen savers, Font*

These pages are devoted to all aspects of chess graphics. There is a massive choice, including paintings, cartoons, woodcuts, lithographs, screen savers, allegorical engravings, daguerreotypes... and ordinary photos as well.

The site invites you to "give your chess pages a classical look with these designs from 'Le Palamède Français' (1863)" and indeed, if you are a Webmaster, this should be your first port of call for those all-important images. The site also mentions that, "all the graphics available at this site are known or believed to be in the public domain". This is important, since most of the pictures of this quality on the Internet belong to copyrighted photo libraries and will cost you £40 or more to use. You can also download 'The Traveller Standard freeware true type chess font' and read details of where to find other fonts and get help with using them.

6) Chessopolis ****
www.chessopolis.com/new.htm

Headers: *Archives/Game Collections, Chess Books & Reviews, Clubs & Organizations, Computer Chess Correspondence & E-mail Chess, Discussion, History/Trivia, Miscellaneous, News, Online Chess, Openings, Players/Bios, Problems, Publications/Newsletters, Shops/Commercial, Software, Tutorials/Lessons, Variants*

This is an excellent collection of links. The only minor drawbacks are that you can't see or print out a list of all the links and it doesn't actually grade sites. On the other hand, the sites all look handpicked and there is usually a concise description with some kind of evaluation included. Also, the extensive list of categories sets this site apart from most of its competitors. Take your pick. Chessopolis is even confident and magnanimous enough to include a section detailing other link collections.

7) ChessPad Homepage *****
www1.tip.nl/~t799997/chesspad.htm

Headers: *ChessPad 1.0 Beta 3 (691K)*, *PGN-registration killing patch*, *Comments*

ChessPad is Mark van der Leek's free chess database program for Windows 95/98/NT. It is meant to be a simple, easy-to-use chess database program, and it is. It can handle large databases of 250,000 games and more, view up to 2000 games in a tree, and will classify openings automatically.

It is outstanding for producing games and diagrams for use on the Web. Firstly, it will output the game score with figurine notation. Secondly, it will produce excellent chess diagrams quickly and easily. They look great, are just the right size and are each made up of 64 tiny square graphics meaning that you can put as many diagrams on a page as you like and it will still download at roughly the same speed. The author has even provided a PGN-registration killing patch, which makes sure that his program won't automatically register itself as your main chess file viewer. If you are thinking of putting chess diagrams on your chess site then download this excellent freeware program.

8) The Chess Show *****
www.teleport.com/~clinto/chessshow/index.html

Headers: *Cybele and Botielus*, *Real Audio/Video Archive*, *Hand crafted earrings by Cybele!*, *Sample tapes now available!*, *Press clipping*, *Schedule (Reruns)*, *Now with Video Conferencing!*, *You Watching Us*, *Who won The Chess Show Internet Chess Tournament?*, *Chess Show Gallery!*, *The Chess Show FAQ*, *Theme Song (387K.au)*

The funniest and most surreal chess site on the Web, *The Chess Show* is "Definitely to be confused with The Cheese Show" and was "Selected, by Willamette Week, as the best public access show in Portland!" Believe it or not, this TV show really does exist for lucky viewers in a tiny corner of Oregon, and the rest of the world can sample highlights by tuning into the Website. According to Special writer, Bill Donahue in *The Oregonian*, chess was once "a dreary game—a game played only by nerds who wore highwater slacks and spent weekends picking the lint out of their slide rules. The story is different now though: Chess is intriguing these days; it is hip... Produced by Portland software engineer Clinton Wittstruck, *The Chess Show* is a zany *Wheel of Fortune* parody. Note, for instance, the hostess, 'The Fabulous Cybele', who gallivants around as viewers phone in to tell her which piece should be moved on the giant chess board superimposed on a studio wall. Cybele wears slinky evening gowns on this monthly program, mimicking the ever-buoyant Vanna White."

The Gallery of photographs offers exhibits such as alien_abduction.jpg, botelius_on_saturn.jpg, cybele+frog.jpg and space_pirate.jpg. If you think these guys are so way out they're on another planet, you could be right, as they display an obsessive fascination with outer space. One of the video clips is a rock song called *Chess on the Moon*, and links to other sites include The UFO Museum and Chess Space. The show is evidently a source of inspiration for some viewers, especially Sally Neal, who sent in a postcard which reads: "Dear Chess Show Players—I've in the past had bad chess experiences, due to a lame boyfriend who always wanted to try king-pawn openings, etc. Thanks to your show I'm no longer threatened by chess, and in fact think I might even learn to play one day. Your show is fantastic, keep up the great work!"

9) The Chess Variant Pages *****
www.chessvariants.com

Headers: *Main index file, On these pages, What's new?, Contributors, Alphabetical index, How you can help, Awards, Recognized Chess Variants*

Pricecheck: *The Chinese Chess Pack US$24.00, Chess Detective: Kriegspiel Strategies, Endgames and Problems $15.00, Stealth Chess $29.99*

If you find chess too easy or you're sick of losing, it may be time for a change. In that case, head straight for The Chess Variant Pages, where you'll find the rules for hundreds of different games, from Chinese Chess and Shogi, to chess with dice, atomic chess (pieces explode when taken), and Goliath chess (pieces can shoot after they have captured). The variants are indexed alphabetically and also by theme: chess on different-sized boards, different opening setups, winning in a different way, moving your opponents' pieces and so on. The Dutch author of this site, Hans Bodlaender, hasn't forgotten plain old 'FIDE' chess. Far from it. He has included 3 pages of chess links, which are especially good for finding chess computer programs and places to play online, against human or computer opponents. This excellent site is updated weekly with new variants that come to light (such as "Three-player hexagonal variant with extra pieces") and plenty more features, programs and comment on Chess Variant Games.

10) Computer Chess Programming *****
www.xs4all.nl/~verhelst/chess/programming.html

Headers: *Reference Material, Programming Techniques, Endgame Databases, Computer Game Research, Computer*

Chess Championships, Chess Programming Information, Chess Programs, Chess Software, Other Computer Chess Pages, Other Computer Games, Miscellaneous

Paul Verhelst from the Netherlands has diligently collected and indexed hundreds of chess programming resources on the Internet, and he also lists books on the subject, which aren't available electronically. Whatever you want to know about chess software—whether you are a computer programmer, a chess player or a problemist—start here. Verhelst describes most of the links so that you don't have to waste time visiting a site to find out what's there. He has also included some work of his own, such as information on how to design chessboard representations. The resolutely non-technical may appreciate Verhelst's links to computer chess championships.

11) The Correspondence Chess Place *****
www.correspondencechess.com

Headers: *Site Philosophy, About Me, An Argument In Favour Of CC, How To Begin Playing CC, The CC Player's Creed, How To Avoid Errors In CC, CC Links—Evaluated, CC Scoresheet—Word 6 Format, Interview With Jon Edwards 10th US CC Champion, CC Archive, 180,000+ Games, CC Hall Of Fame, The Game Of Chess, CC In The Year 2010, The Two Faces Of CC, Computer Use In CC, Thirty Great Combos, How I Almost Made The 11th USCCC Final, Check Printed Analysis, Book And Software Reviews, Annotated CC Games, Images From Thun, The CC Games Of David C Heap, CC Quotations, Previously Published Articles, No Napoleonic Chess Player On An Air Cushion, Chess Is War!, EXLAM!, Email CC, CC Humor, The Top Ten List, Computers And CC, Public Service Announcements, ICCM Sture Nyman Book—work in progress, The CC Museum*

Pricecheck: *Correspondence Chess World CD US$40.00 excluding postage, MegaCorr CD $24.00, Subscription to* Chess Mail £29.00 (Irish or Sterling)

Updating The Correspondence Chess Place must be a full-time job for John C. Knudsen. Big doesn't always mean beautiful, but in this case, breadth and depth are matched by professionalism and enthusiasm. If you are already a CC player, you will think you've reached heaven when you look at this site. If you haven't yet experienced the joys of this perfectionist form of chess, you may well be tempted to try it out after reading some of Knudsen's articles. Sceptics argue that CC has been killed off by computers, but Knudsen is dismissive of this suggestion, giving 10 reasons not to use computers. As he points out, you'll have to share the glory with your machine if you win or draw.

Nowadays, CC can be played by e-mail as well as snail mail, and Knudsen offers masters the chance to enter his own e-mail tournaments, exclusively for players rated over 2200. There is no entry fee: these tournaments are designed for people who would like to play via the Internet but have problems with currency exchange. For non-masters, Knudsen's site is a treasure trove of interesting games, discussions and CC resources. A vast selection of chess books can be purchased online in conjunction with Internet bookshop Amazon, and Knudsen also offers several books for downloading electronically. The site also hosts the renowned Campbell Report (see review in News chapter).

12) Diaz Cartoons ****
ourworld.compuserve.com/homepages/diaz_cartoons

Headers: *The Wimbledon of Chess—Cartoon report on Linares 1999, Chess personalities, Chess topicalities, Chess in the nineties, Chess cartoons on postcards, Chess and computers, Chess comic strip, Chess for...*

Pricecheck: *A limited edition set of four different full-colour postcards on the Kasparov-Deep Blue rematch US$5.00 per set, 15 different black-and-white postcards with Rooky and Chessy cartoons $0.75 per card and $10.00 per set*

Enigmatic cartoonist José Diaz, or José Angel Diaz Criado, to give him his full name, prefers to keep a low profile in the chess world, letting his work speak for itself. Many famous chess players would not recognise Diaz, but he is certainly watching them, recording their gestures and expressions in his memory to reproduce them later in hilarious fashion. Since 1990, he has been drawing chess cartoons, which have appeared in the world's leading magazines, often on the front cover; and he is the author of the 'Rooky and Chessy' comic strip. On this site we are treated to a selection of Diaz's best cartoons, including a besotted Najdorf dancing with a chess queen as her jealous king looks on; J.H. Donner in full kingly regalia with a chequered coat-of-arms on his shield and a pen as a sword; BBC commentators desperate to hear positive news from Nigel Short's friend Dominic Lawson, about the Englishman's chances in his match with Kasparov; and human spectators avidly watching the 2010 world championship—between two computers.

13) InternetChess.com ***
www.Internetchess.com

Headers: *Chess Link Categories, Chess File Downloads, Chess Books, Chess Tactics*

Pricecheck: *Banner advertisement US$8.00/1000 impressions (min. 5000 impressions), Jon Speelman's Best Games $19.16, My System: 21st Century Edition $14.00*

InternetChess.com must be the biggest collection of chess links on the Web, with 42 different categories of links, plus 'All Links', if you want to print them all out for perusal. The best sites in each category have a special symbol beside them, as do the best sites on the entire Web, which according to InternetChess.com are: The Correspondence Chess Place, Chess Café, Inside Chess Online, Internet Chess Club, The Chess Lab, Lost Boys Chess Page, and The Week in Chess. Some of the links have a brief description of the site, but obviously there isn't time to look at every link listed. Annoyingly, they aren't always updated when a site disappears or its URL changes, so some links are dead ends. However, the site is one to watch, because it has also started hosting big events, such as the 'World Championship' match between Kasparov and Kramnik.

14) Jon Levitt's Chess Pages ****
www.jlevitt.dircon.co.uk

Headers: *Are you a chess genius?, Levitt on chess (Selected writings), Games, Studies and Problems, Do not adjust your chess set2, Me and my mates*

Pricecheck: Secrets of Spectacular Chess *and* Genius in Chess *£25.00 post free in the UK, £1.00 p&p in Europe, £2.00 rest of the world*, Fischer-Spassky, The $5,000,000 Comeback *£10.00 plus same postage, Web page design by Tinni Levitt from £20.00 per page*

An enterprising site from a British grandmaster who prides himself on originality of thinking. Levitt manages to promote himself and his books, whilst keeping visitors occupied solving problems, playing through games or admiring the entertaining photos. Certainly the picture of 'Tony Miles, tea lady', is worth its weight in gold. Lengthy extracts from Levitt's books give readers ample opportunity to decide whether to buy them or not, and provide food for thought at the same time. You will soon find out if you are a chess genius, by attempting the speed test in which a knight must visit a number of squares on the board whilst avoiding the enemy queen. If you can't work out how to get to the first square, you can safely assume you are not a chess genius. More controversially, Levitt expounds his views on the correlation between Elo rating and IQ. This will appeal to strong chess players who want to prove they are intelligent, and to people who like to believe that intelligence can be quantified numerically.

15) The Losing Chess Pages *****
ourworld.compuserve.com/homepages/Stan_Goldovski/Index.htm

Headers: *What's new?, Alphabetical index, The rules of Losing Chess, Losing Chess strategy and theory, Problems,*

Studies, Examples, Chess servers supporting Losing Chess, Best players, Events and history, Books and periodicals, Organizations, Losing Chess software, Miscellaneous

It's depressing to realise that being bad at winning chess doesn't necessarily mean you'll be good at Losing Chess. Irritatingly, people who are good at winning chess are probably also good at Losing Chess, which is often called Suicide Chess. Any illusions that Losing Chess is a childish game involving silly moves are dispelled by this site. Losing Chess games (where it is compulsory to capture and the winner is the first person to lose all their pieces) are analysed here in exactly the same depth as conventional chess. Losing Chess can give you an extraordinarily big headache, for instance when you have to work out which piece your opponent will promote their pawn to. You might get so fed up with it that you feel like committing suicide!

Ratings for Losing Chess can be obtained by playing on Internet chess servers, and several people already have ratings over 2200. Some of them have contributed analyses of their games to this site, so a body of theory on the subject is developing at quite a pace. The site does everything possible to teach the rules to newcomers and provide interesting material for more advanced players. Even if you hate losing, it doesn't matter, because losing is winning. And if you get tired of winning (or losing) against humans at the game, you can download a computer opponent. Although the Webmaster's ill health has restricted him from updating The Losing Chess Pages regularly, this is still a great site.

16) Manolis Stratakis Chess Problem Page *****
www.forthnet.gr/chess

Headers: *Submitted Problems, Unusual Problems, Openings, Checkmates, MS Problems, Competition, Hall of Fame, Other Problems, Books, Software, Web Play, Acknowledgment*

Visitors to this site are greeted by a tiny map and the legend, "This page is physically located in Heraklio, Crete, Greece"—a nice touch, typical of this pleasant, action-packed site. There are all sorts of chess problems here and they have been split into interesting and well-written sections. Extravagant hyperlinks such as, 'The White King Looks At The Black Rooks And Laughs!! Can You See Why?' make you click out of curiosity. The challenge, 'White Moves And ... Does Not Checkmate The Black!', teases us into attempting this apparently easy task. Once you have solved any or all of the problems, you can e-mail your answer/s to Manolis and get yourself on the 'Hall of Fame' page. There are even some rather good problems composed by the Webmaster himself, and a link to submit your own or your favourites. For light relief and for people who want to return to the 'real' chess world, the 'Spectacular Miniatures Gallery' has some interesting games by 'Old Masters' that ended quickly and carry the challenge, 'What Happened Next?'

17) Randy's Revealing Reviews *****
ourworld.compuserve.com/homepages/randybauer
Headers: *What's New?, Reviews, Instructive Games, Chess Tips, About the Author*

A fantastic site, immaculately produced so that it is super-quick to navigate and enjoyable to read. No unnecessary frames or gimmicky features such as sound effects. The purpose of the site is also clear: "It's said that there are more books written about chess than all other games combined. Coupled with the explosion of computer chess products, it's often hard for the average player to know what is good and useful and what is not. I hope to help provide that guidance," says Bauer. Alongside his impressive list of meaty book reviews, in which all the books are given a rating on a scale of 0-10, Bauer also offers free chess instruction for club players and some well-presented chess links that he recommends.

Bauer himself is a US National Chess Master from Iowa rated 2304 ("the highest rated Iowa player on the USCF's 1997 annual rating list"!), who gives chess lessons to his bearded collie Duffy when he can't get anyone else to listen—a photo confirms that Duffy is an attentive student!

18) Tim Krabbé's Chess Curiosities ****
www.xs4all.nl/~timkr/chess/chess.html
Open chess diary, AD-Magazine Weekly chess column, Games page, The 110 Greatest Moves ever played. Master Jacobson, Chess records, Diagram of the century, Striker grandmaster, A genius' bad luck, Dream combination, The ultimate blunder, Strangest coincidence ever—or hoax?, De Ronde—NN, Migrating to the South, Alekhine's five Queen game, Loman's move, Jan Timman, and the double Prokes, A walk with Gary Kasparov, The Full Morphy, The discovery of the Saavedra, A love story with a diagram, Willi Schlage On Fischer, The Platypussy Trap, The Intergalactic Chess Café, Stiller's Monsters or Perfection in Chess, Dear Pitt Chess Club, Pawn in reverse Check!, A Tragedy in Elista, Two moves by Geller, Probleemjaren Makruk, In storm and rain, Chess quotes, Comments, suggestions, Questions, Bio- & bibliography

Film buffs will know Tim Krabbé as the man who wrote the screenplay for *The Vanishing*, which was based on his own novel; chess players may know him as a strong opponent over the board, or as a problem composer. He is also the author of the acclaimed *Chess Curiosities*. Krabbé is a Webmaster, too, bringing his favorite games and problems to life with the help of Java, and telling stories about his memorable moments in chess.

Playing Anand in a blindfold clock simul, he was distracted by thoughts of the beautiful girl he had slept with the night before, but still managed to draw. In 'The Intergalactic Chess Café', Krabbé describes his addiction to playing chess on ICC, which started in the days when there was no graphical interface and moves had to be made on a real set. Krabbé also publishes here (with Bobby Fischer's permission) the full text of that classic pamphlet from 1981, 'I was tortured in the Pasadena Jailhouse!' On the quotes page, we discover that Mikhail Botvinnik only ever played one blitz game, on a train in 1929. Krabbé has also persisted in his "until now fruitless search in non-chess publications for chessboards with a light square in the right-hand corner". A wonderfully varied site.

19) Tim Mann's Chess Page ***
www.research.digital.com/SRC/personal/Tim_Mann/chess.html

Headers: *XBoard and WinBoard, GNU Chess, Crafty, Internet Chess Servers, Zippy, Bughouse. Chess Web Sites, Chess FTP Sites, Chess Discussion Groups, Linking to PGN files*

Computer fanatics can download chess engines here with names like: Comet, The Crazy Bishop, La Dame Blanche, and the more well-known Crafty; you can also download graphical interfaces for playing chess via the Internet against human opponents. Mann provides some technical information of his own on the chess program, GNU Chess. Otherwise, the site mainly consists of links to other chess sites, including bughouse sites (or exchange chess, as the British call it). You can make contact with "someone who plays e-mail correspondence bughouse". Some mothers do 'ave 'em.

20) Traveller Chess Sites ****
www3.traveller.com/chess

Headers: *The Chess Archives, Huntsville Chess Club, Swiss Perfect, Author's comments, How to link to this page*

Pricecheck: *Swiss Perfect US$49.00, plus $5.00 for mail and handling within the US or $15.00 rest of the world*

This is a fascinating, if disorganised, collection of chess sites put together by someone called David Hayes, who was joint Alabama correspondence champion in 1994. His correspondence rating at the time was 1975, which is relevant, as he offers coaching by e-mail for US$20/hour.

Hayes' views on chess are highly personal and idiosyncratic, which adds to the charm of the site, but at the same time can be annoying, depending on your mood. Under the heading, 'The Zen of Chess', he dispenses pretentious quasi-philosophical advice such as, "Go into chess as young as possible. Bring all the assets you have and play to win. Chess is a remarkable game. If you saturate yourself with chess, then the game will all but take you by the hand and point the way."

It's not going to win any design awards, but this is a site with something for everyone. There is a large collection of chess-related graphics, and an easy to use 'Chess Diagram Construction Device'. Hayes' pages for beginners offer advice on rules, chess terminology and basic endings; a few of his best games are introduced with a stanza from Tennyson's *Charge of the Light Brigade*, which aptly sets the scene for some violent confrontations.

The openings library is rather limited at the moment—the only opening covered is 1 g4—but the notorious Grob is explored in considerable depth, with the aid of diagrams, and Hayes promises to expand this section in future. Other sites that come under the Traveller umbrella, include the 5-Piece Endgame Solution Server and the Chess Problem Server, massive databases which can be searched for the solutions to millions of positions. The 5-Piece Endgame Solution Server is particularly useful for any unfinished games you have. It works back from checkmate to any position involving five pieces or less. It will play it perfectly. There is also a limited implementation of a 6-Piece Solution Server. Lets hope it doesn't get to 32 pieces too quickly! Food for thought2 and there is even some real food on offer in the form of 'Chess Recipes'. Why not try 'Buttermilk Chess Pie', 'Pineapple-Coconut Chess Pie', 'Afterthought Lemon Chess' or 'Chocolate Chess Tarts'?

Huntsville Chess Club challenges the world to matches by e-mail, and Swiss Perfect is an advertisement for a tournament administration computer program.

21) Vishwanathan Anand Chess Pages *****
http://www.geocities.com/Colosseum/Slope/4448
Headers: *Vishwanathan Anand's 2000 Schedule, Biographies, Vishy Anand in the media, AnandWatch, Anand Career Stats, AnandBase, Puzzles, Picture Gallery*

If you are a fan of Anand, then rush to this site. It's kept bang up to date and follows his progress daily when he's in a tournament. You can have up-to-the-minute information sent to your inbox about his upcoming, recent and past appearances by joining the e-mail list. There is a well-ordered collection of biographical notes on Anand and his chess career, and an excellent collection of links. The site also acts as a home for, as it states on the site, the "many, many articles on Anand and his interviews that appear on the Web... but disappear all too soon". AnandBase is a compilation of Anand's games. All of his 1999 games are here and earlier years are promised soon. Most files are in PGN format, but there are also some rather fun animated games that you can just sit back with a cup of tea and marvel at. The quality is already here on this young site, the quantity is sure to follow.

D/ Newsgroups

1) *alt.chess* **

They have snaffled the best name, but this newsgroup is not highly frequented, as evidenced by the plaintive cry from an anonymous e-mailer, "Is anyone reading my postings?" If your query is urgent, make sure this isn't the only place where you post it. Nevertheless, of the few postings you'll find, most will elicit some response.

2) *alt.chess.bdg* *

This newsgroup seems to consist mainly of endless debates about the philosophy of chess, winning, losing, all sorts of weird and sensible stuff here. Quite fun, but don't come here to find raw data.

3) *alt.chess.ics* *

Not a massive newsgroup but people do respond to postings and it is mostly chess-related. From the evidence here already, if you are a beginner, you will most likely get a good response to anything you ask here.

4) *gnu.chess* ***

"The newsgroup gnu.chess and the mailing list *info-gnu-chess@gnu.org* are for the discussion of GNU Chess, XBoard, and related free chess software," says Tim Mann on his Website. The talk on the newsgroup at the time of writing was about 'Blue Gene', which will apparently be 1,000 times more powerful than the Deep Blue machine that defeated world champion Garry Kasparov in 1997. It would also be some two million times more powerful than the current top-of-the-line desktops. A good newsgroup if you are a chess programmer, or if you are interested in computer chess.

5) *rec.games.chess* *

Practically everything here has been posted by people who are sending their messages to every single chess newsgroup, so there is nothing that you won't find at *rec.games.chess.misc.*

6) *rec.games.chess.computer* *****

This newsgroup is an excellent place to go if you are interested in chess computers. It covers everything from new software for small pocket organisers to current Computer vs Master chess matches.

7) *rec.games.chess.misc* *****

A hugely popular newsgroup, covering everything under the sun: from women in chess, to tournament results, beginners' books, FIDE politics, the laws of chess, personalities of chess players, and chess with vodka. Around 250 new messages are posted every week, and many of them include links to Websites where even more information can be found.

Steve Pribut posts his lengthy FAQ document (frequently asked questions) twice a month here and on *rec.games.chess*, advising which books improving players should buy, how to play chess by e-mail and which chess magazines are available.

8) *rec.games.chess.politics* ****

Any aspect of chess politics can be discussed here, although it is dominated by Americans who have strong opinions about the USCF. Kirsan Ilyumzhinov, FIDE ratings and Bobby Fischer are also popular subjects. Well-known names such as Sam Sloan, Tim Krabbé, Larry Parr, 'Mig', and Tryfon Gavriel have contributed to the group at one time or another (many times, in the case of Sloan and Parr).

E/ Mailing Lists

1) ChessChat *****
ChessChat-subscribe@egroups.com

This is a fun group. People post each other chess problems and know each other by name. There is also a 'chess by turns' game going, which involves a number of people. Joining this group will get you about six or seven e-mails a day of an interesting chess nature and people take the time to write quite long postings. An example of the type of posting you might read: "Here are some alternatives to the normal (i.e. ! = Good move ? = Bad move) type of annotations including... $ The player is thinking about the prize money, $- Since the player is thinking about the prize money, he will lose, +=- The player had a winning position and then a draw, but is now losing, S The player has been swindled. SX The player has been swindled and is cross about it. @ The player is a dot-com millionaire."

2) Chess-L ***
CHESS-L@NIC.SURFNET.NL

Chess politics and top-level tournaments are the main topics of this group, although nothing is discussed in depth. Sam Sloan posts his latest findings here, such as the Federal Grand Jury Indictment of Bobby Fischer for sanctions-busting. Contributions to Chess-L are fairly sparse and occasionally entertaining, so at least you won't be bombarded with utter junk if you subscribe.

3) Lancashire Chess Discussion List ***
mailserver@lancashirechess.demon.co.uk

This list doesn't have too many subscribers. However, the postings are of good quality, so joining it won't fill your inbox full of junk. You will find gentle discussion of the new laws of chess, a few chess problems and the latest chess results.

10 Secrets of Chess Webmastery

by John Saunders

The first question for you, the aspirant chess Webmaster, is: "Do you really, really, really want to set up and maintain a chess Website?" Unless your answer to this question is an unequivocal, positively maniacal, "YES!", then we are all wasting our time here. And it still has to be "Yes" tomorrow, next week, week in week out, month after month. The key word in the question is "maintain". The Internet thrives on novelty. All the time that the reader looks at your page, he or she will looking for tell-tale signs that the Webmaster has updated recently and is likely to do so in the not too distant future. Will this be a site worth visiting every day or two, or maybe every week? Or are there the all-too-frequent give-away signs indicating that the site was set up in a wild burst of enthusiasm, but has not been updated since? People like Websites, not dead sites. So the secret of Webmastery is revealed already—it's regular, hard work. Or as Webgrandmaster Mark Crowther once said to me: "Welcome to the masochistic world of daily chess journalism!"

So we can now take it as read that the Webmaster is ready, with a story to tell, and determined to do the hard graft of periodic updates. What materials are needed? The specification of PC is not important; anything that is good enough to connect you to the Internet and can load up Web pages should be good enough for Web page editing. You will of course need to sign up with an Internet service provider (ISP). Quite a lot of ISPs these days make available to their users a fixed amount of Web space in which the user can set up their own Web pages. This can vary from 3 to 20 megabytes. It is surprising how much can be fitted onto a few megabytes. To use your free Web space it is usually just a question of sending an e-mail to the ISP saying, "I want to use my free 5 megabytes, please." They will then set it up and give you a password for uploading files. That's pretty well all there is to getting the space you need. If your ISP is mean and doesn't give away free space—or is one of those annoying ones that insists on splashing its adverts all over your screen whether you like it or not—there are now a number of sites where you can get free Web space. There are a few strings attached, of course, such as the right to send you e-mail 'spam' at regular intervals, but at least this doesn't inconvenience your readers.

So you've got your computer, Internet connection, and some disk space waiting for you to hold your Web pages. Now we have to write those Web pages. This process is similar to word processing. You can purchase expensive Web authoring tools but it is often possible to use the WP software that you already have. The latest versions of products like **Microsoft Word** allow you to save WP files as HTML (Hypertext Markup Language) files. If you save a file in this mode—without doing anything particularly clever, you have created a Web page. It will have a suffix of .HTM or .HTML and it is ready to be loaded into a browser. Try loading it up using your usual Internet browser to see what the file looks like.

Here's where you will probably need to take some time to experiment and learn, by trying out different formats and layouts. You will need to think about the design of your page and look at what other people do on their Websites. If you like someone's site layout, you can technically (though not necessarily legally!) download their page to your hard disk and have a look at how they design their page using your Web page editor.

It is probably too early to think about investing in a professional Webmastering package, though some of these are relatively inexpensive even for the beginner. A better approach is to browse the Internet for shareware or freeware Web authoring tools. There is a wide selection of such tools available at Internet software sites. One recommended site is the well-known 'Tucows' site at http://tucows.cablenet.co.uk— this has a very well indexed selection of shareware/freeware tools that can be appraised and downloaded. Another approach is to check out the site where your browser came from, to see if they provide add-ons for editing. For example, there is a version of Netscape Navigator called Netscape Navigator Gold, which contains a very useful Web authoring and uploading facility, freely downloadable from the Netscape site.

A slight digression is called for here. If you download files from the Internet, sooner or later you are going to need another piece of utility software to help you 'unpack' your downloaded items. This is a file compression/decompression utility, or what is more commonly known as a 'zip' or 'unzip' package. Many downloads are compressed (or zipped) to reduce download times and allow several files to be transmitted in one package. Once the file has been downloaded, it needs to be unzipped to reveal its contents and (for example) make a piece of software ready for use. There are several such shareware utilities available around the Web, with well-known ones being **Winzip** and **PKZIP**. You will need to have just such a utility ready to go on your computer before you start using software downloaded from Tucows and other sites.

Take plenty of time to become acquainted with your chosen Web authoring tool. Your Website will benefit from graphics and photographs. For these purposes, a scanner or a digital camera can be invaluable. To turn the scanned or digital image into something that your browser can handle, you are also going to need some software to turn the bitmap image into a 'jpg' or 'gif' file, which are basically image formats used on the Internet. Again the Internet itself is a great source of image editors that can do this job for you; call in at Tucows and you should find a few. One well-known one is **Paintshop Pro**. Download it and play with it, and soon you should be ready to insert them into your Web page in appropriate places. When editing your image, think about the size of the resultant file. Keep the image below 50k in size, or your readers may get fed up waiting for the image to load and abscond to another site. Finally, for the same reason, don't put too many images on the same Web page.

Do consider buying or borrowing a digital camera. Prices are coming down all the time, and the good news is that you do not have to buy a top-of-the-range model in order to produce acceptable images for your Website. A high-resolution capability is simply not necessary for Web-based images; it is only useful for photography buffs who want to produce high-quality prints from digital images, or have images printed in newspapers and magazines. You will be amazed at how easy it is to take a picture and transfer it to your computer. But the editing process can be time-consuming until you know your way around the image editing software. As well as **Paintshop Pro**, you might consider **Ulead Photoimpact**, which has an easy-to-use facility for the production of 'jpg' and 'gif' files for Web use. You may find that your 'free' downloaded image editing package stops working after a predetermined trial period, but in all probability your camera will come with a free image editing software package anyway, which should provide reasonable facilities for the production of Web images.

Let's assume that you have written your home page with details of (say) your chess club, contact details, venue, etc, with a prominent, scanned-in picture of the club cat, Capablanca, and are ready to publish (or 'upload', as it is usually referred to). You need another bit of software, called an 'ftp' program. That stands for File Transfer Protocol. Once again, you can get one for free (or not very much) by looking on the Internet. A good one is **WS-FTP** but there are many equally good ones. This software does the job of transferring copies of your files from the directory where you keep them on your computer to the ISP's disk server. Before doing this, your connection to your ISP will need to be switched on. And you will need the exact details that your ISP gave you when you asked for the free Web space connection. They will probably send you an explanatory e-mail giving a few details of how you connect to their site for Web uploading. If they don't, ask. As for your FTP software, it will probably be possible to configure it so that it remembers the addresses on your computer and the ISP, so that you don't have to look them up the next time. It can probably also be programmed with the password that you use to upload so that you don't have to key it in every time you update. But do make a careful, handwritten note of the ISP address and password and keep it somewhere safe and secure—you will need it again at some point.

Once your page has been uploaded to the ISP's disk space, it is now readable by the whole world. Technically your job is done until the next time you need to update. But it is a very good idea to connect to the site to load the page yourself, in order to test it. It is amazing how often that something that seemed to work fine on your own computer suddenly looks like a disaster area when uploaded to the Web. Common reasons are links to images that have been incorrectly specified, or links to files which you have forgotten to upload or are named differently to the link identifier.

Another chess-related problem is the business of figurine fonts. These look marvellous on your own machine, but other people find a meaningless mass of squiggles on their screens unless they happen to have the same set of specialist fonts as you. Even then, fancy fonts can get lost in transit. Note that filenames on the Internet are case sensitive, and this is also a very frequent cause of broken links and errant images. Remember to test any links to external pages to see if they work. If you run a 'links' page, it is also good practice to go back and test it periodically. Inevitably one or two of your links will no longer work as people's Websites go defunct or move to new locations, or, horror of horrors, you may find that what used to be a link to the Trumpton Chess Club, is now advertising something unsavoury or illegal!

That's enough technical detail. After a while you should have enough expertise to be able to put together a few reasonably designed Web pages that link together successfully. Now—what about your material? There are lots of chess-related pages on the Web, with a multiplicity of themes, such as selling things, celebrating famous players, providing local, national or international chess news, giving away downloadable databases or chess-related software, advertising tournaments or clubs, collections of photographs.

There really is no limit. Perhaps the best way to start is to think about what information you have access to which is unique and can form the basis of a chess Web page. Very often this will be details about your own chess club. Even if all you have to say about your club is where and when it meets and a contact name and phone number, it is worth setting up the page. This is perhaps an exception to the rule about regular updating; so long as the details remain the same, there is no need to update the site regularly, if all you are trying to achieve is a free advert similar to a notice in the newsagent's window. But one thing you should do after setting up the site, is to get your site registered on search engines (such as AltaVista or Yahoo!) so that people can find your site. Give it a simple but meaningful title such as Trumpton Chess Club Web Site. That way, someone who moves to the area and wants to find the local chess club can type "Trumpton chess" into the search engine, and bingo!, up pops your Website on their screen.

Now you will need to spend some time hawking your Website around the best chess links pages. *New in Chess* magazine has a very good one and if your club is British you should mail Tryfon Gavriel who runs the excellent BritWeb site. He will put up your club's name on his site and you will get some useful, and free, publicity. Make sure you return the compliment by linking back to BritWeb. Other countries have similar sites which group together all the national chess sites and help people to find a place to play chess in the vicinity. Generally you should budget about 10-20 per cent of your time spent setting up a Website on promotion. E-mail your friends and acquaintances, telling them that the site exists and what it is all about; go to one of the chess-related newsgroups (such as *rec.games.chess.misc*) and advertise it briefly (don't forget to mention the address!); and check out similar sites and offer to exchange links with them. If they do subsequently link to your site, make sure you keep to your offer by reciprocating. Generally you will find that chess Webmasters are a friendlier breed than chess players and do their best to help each other out when they can. There isn't a 'Chess Webmasters' Union' yet, but it is only a matter of time.

There are lots of other reasons for setting up a chess Website and you will be limited only by your imagination, your creativity and your writing skills. The secret is: get ready to do it, start doing it, and then keep doing it!